Austerity justice

Steve Hynes is the director of Legal Action Group (LAG). Previously he was the director of Law Centres Federation, the national organisation for Law Centres, and worked as co-ordinator at Rochdale Law Centre where he also undertook casework in employment and discrimination law.

Available as an ebook at www.lag.org.uk/ebooks

The purpose of the Legal Action Group is to promote equal access to justice for all members of society who are socially, economically or otherwise disadvantaged. To this end, it seeks to improve law and practice, the administration of justice and legal services.

Austerity justice

Steve Hynes

Legal Action Group
2012

This edition published in Great Britain 2012
by LAG Education and Service Trust Limited
242 Pentonville Road, London N1 9UN
www.lag.org.uk

British Library Cataloguing in Publication Data
a CIP catalogue record for this book is available from the British Library.

Crown copyright material is produced with the permission of the
Controller of HMSO and the Queen's Printer for Scotland.

This book has been produced using Forest Stewardship
Council®(FSC®) certified paper. The wood used to produce
FSC certified products with a 'Mixed Sources' label comes
from FSC certified well-managed forests, controlled sources
and/or recycled material.

FSC
www.fsc.org
MIX
Paper from
responsible sources
FSC® C020438

Print ISBN   978 1 908407 20 7
ebook ISBN   978 1 908407 21 4

Typeset by Regent Typesetting, London
Printed in Great Britain by Hobbs the Printers, Totton, Hampshire

Acknowledgments

This book is dedicated to all the organisations and people who were part of the Justice for All campaign and the wider opposition against the legal aid proposals in the Legal Aid, Sentencing and Punishment of Offenders Act 2012. Many are mentioned in the following pages, but I apologise for any omissions.

I would like to thank the people who agreed to be interviewed for this book. Some wished to remain anonymous, but their insight and knowledge has contributed greatly to my understanding of how legal aid and access to justice policy has arrived at this point (you know who you are!).

Thanks to Vicky Ling and Carol Storer for commenting on draft chapters and to Esther Pilger, publisher, and all of the staff and board members at Legal Action Group (LAG).

The early chapters draw on interviews and research I undertook for *The Justice Gap: whatever happened to legal aid?* (LAG, 2009) which I co-authored with Jon Robins.

Finally, thanks to Tom Dunn and Roger Leese at Clifford Chance and for the firm's financial support for this book.

Contents

APPENDICES

The peaks and troughs of legal aid

This book marks the 40th anniversary of the founding of Legal Action Group (LAG). In November 1971, four lawyers called a meeting which was attended by about 80 advisers, lawyers and academics. The aim was to raise money for an information service and to monitor the delivery of legal services around the country. This meeting led to the launch of LAG and the *LAG Bulletin* in 1972. The *LAG Bulletin* became the *Legal Action* journal, and we branched out in our early years into books and training courses. These have been very successful in assisting practitioners both in private practice and the not-for-profit sector become more expert in areas of work which are important to the poor and other vulnerable people. This book sets out a brief history of the legal aid system with an emphasis on civil legal aid, as well as the contribution of pro bono and not-for-profit services in providing access to justice to the public. LAG has been intimately involved in chronicling this history and influencing policy in this field throughout its 40 years of existence.

It was in the early 1970s that a number of important advances were made in access to justice, such as the commencement of what became known as the 'green form' legal aid scheme and the establishment of the first Law Centres. Much of LAG's policy work over the years has been aimed at building on these innovations to open up access to justice for the public. In our 20th anniversary year we published *A strategy for justice*.[1] In this book LAG set out the problems and solutions to providing accessible publicly funded legal services.

One of the central ideas of *A strategy for justice* was to suggest that a coherent method was needed to plan the provision of legal services. A legal services commission was proposed to take over from

1 *A strategy for justice*, LAG, 1992.

the then Legal Aid Board, and local planning of legal advice services was suggested. Both of these ideas were adopted, but with mixed success. The development by the Labour government of 1997–2010 of Community Legal Service Partnerships to better plan and co-ordinate services was along the lines which LAG had proposed. They met with mixed success and were abandoned to save costs. As for the Legal Services Commission, this was established by the last government, but as discussed later, its demise is now imminent.

Peter Chandler, one of the founders of the Law Centre movement, a long-time LAG supporter and still-practising legal aid solicitor, put it succinctly when he said we were going to have 'to fight again the battles of forty years ago'. Peter Chandler is right to be pessimistic. In legal aid and access to justice policy we have had our peaks and troughs over these years (though at the time we have often failed to recognise the peaks). The impending cuts to legal aid introduced through the Legal Aid, Sentencing and Punishment of Offenders (LASPO) Act 2012 will be by any measure the most far-reaching in the scheme's history, and will have a profound impact on access to justice for the general public. Some of the answers as to why state support for publicly funded legal services has reached such a low point pre-date the current coalition government, but this should not detract from the low-point that LASPO represents.

After the general election in May 2010, Britain got its first coalition government in 70 years. While the option of a Labour and Liberal Democrat coalition might have been a better political fit, it just did not have the numbers of MPs to work. The Conservatives were the biggest party in the House of Commons with 306 MPs, and with the Liberal Democrats winning 57 seats at the election, a government could be formed with a viable working majority over Labour and the other parties.

The coalition government faced then – and still does at the time of writing, more than two years later – an extremely grim economic outlook due to the recession caused in large part by the banking crisis of 2008/09. At the centre of the government's policy is the aim to cut government expenditure in order to reduce the public spending deficit, and this has been reiterated in the latest budget statement of 2012.[2] Opinion is divided on whether the policy will have the desired effect. What seems certain is that the austerity policies will be with us a while longer than the government had originally intended. It is clear that the British economy, and the world economy in general,

2   See budget statement from HM Treasury, 21 March 2012.

are taking more time to recover than was first envisaged. Chancellor of the Exchequer, George Osborne, warned in November 2011 that: 'Instability across the world and in our main export markets means that, in common with many other countries, expectations for this year's growth have fallen.'[3]

A crucial part of the deal that brought the current government into being was the painstakingly negotiated coalition agreement. This was thrashed out between the two partners in the days after the general election and was published on 20 May 2010.

Compromises in government are inevitable, as politicians have to grapple with multi-faceted problems for which pragmatic, as opposed to ideological, solutions are often more likely to be successful. The section of the coalition agreement on justice seems to be inspired by a particularly heavy dose of political pragmatism. It promises a 'rehabilitation revolution' which, as well as being in keeping with the political impulses of many Liberal Democrats, would have the advantage of reducing prison numbers and therefore the largest cost-driver in the Ministry of Justice's budget. The then Justice Secretary, Kenneth Clarke, when a green paper on sentencing was published in December 2010, talked about reducing the 85,500 prison population by 3,000 by 2014.[4]

In the first days of the coalition, with announcements such as this it did seem that on justice policy the government was leaning towards a more liberal civil liberties agenda. In addition to the 'rehabilitation revolution', the government announced the scrapping of the national identity card scheme, or 'laminated poll tax' as it had been dubbed by the then Liberal Democrat Shadow Home Secretary, Chris Huhne, in 2008. This was another political move which had the dual advantage of both being in line with the junior coalition partner's policies, as well as contributing towards the deficit reduction by saving money. The coalition agreement also promised 'a Freedom or Great Repeal Bill' to reform libel law and the Freedom of Information Act 2000, to restore rights to non-violent protest and to give greater protection over the DNA database.[5]

---

3   8 November 2011. www.hm-treasury.gov.uk/statement_dx_11001.htm.
4   Alan Travis and Helene Mulholland, 'Prison system failing to tackle reoffending, says Ken Clarke', *Guardian*, 7 December 2010, available at: www.guardian.co.uk/politics/2010/dec/07/prison-failing-tackle-reoffending-ken-clarke.
5   Philip Johnston, 'New government's Great Repeal Bill can help repair Labour's damage to our liberties', *Telegraph*, 12 May 2010, available at: http://blogs.telegraph.co.uk/news/philipjohnston/100039561/new-governments-great-repeal-bill-can-help-repair-labours-damage-to-our-liberties/.

What is emerging is a tendency from the government to opt for savings in the justice budget (perhaps with the exception of penal policy), which by coincidence rather than design are in keeping with the civil liberties instincts of Liberal Democrats and some Conservatives. However, when it comes to spending choices to support civil justice, the coalition has opted for draconian cuts behind the smoke-screen of deficit reduction. A combination of careless policy-making and a blatant disregard for the needs for the poor and vulnerable means that the government is at risk of creating a rights deficit at the heart of the civil justice system in the UK.

The proposal contained in the coalition agreement to hold a fundamental review of the legal aid system, as well not being an original idea, embodied the government's flawed approach to justice, as it was mainly concerned with finding cuts to contribute to the deficit reduction with no regard to their wider consequences. Civil justice, specifically family and social welfare law, emerged as the biggest losers from this review. This was owing to a combination of factors which this book examines, some of which pre-date the present government – for example, the tension between the criminal and civil parts of the legal aid system.

Understanding the development of legal aid policy alone does not give the full story on why there is a shortfall in civil legal advice services. Many of these services, particularly those in social welfare law, developed outside the legal aid system through not-for-profit and other mainly non-lawyer led advice services. Not-for-profit services, as discussed later, became a parallel service which had an impact on the development of the legal aid system. This culminated in the opening-up of legal aid contracting widely to the not-for-profit sector under the last government. With this innovation, such services have become more dependent on legal aid funding, but the consequence of this is that they and the people they serve are in danger of falling victim to serious collateral damage from the coalition's cuts to civil legal aid.

What public debate there is about legal aid tends to concentrate on the cost of the system, and on lawyers' remuneration in particular. Successive governments have used this to justify cutbacks in legal aid. The perversity at the heart of legal aid policy is that such reductions have not usually come at price of reducing what lawyers are paid to provide the service, but at the expense of access to justice for the public, especially those least likely to be able to afford to pay for legal advice and representation. It is for these people that LAG argues that current and future governments need to re-think legal aid and access to justice policy.

CHAPTER 1

The big society – civil legal advice prior to 1949

Pro bono services – introduction

Until the Legal Aid Act 1949 there was no legal aid available in civil cases – the majority of the population had no option but to rely on pro bono services for advice and representation. The pro bono movement is important in the story of the development of legal aid, as it demonstrated the need for legal advice services in civil law. When it became clear that demand was outstripping the supply of pro bono backed services, it acted as a catalyst for building political pressure for state-funded civil legal services.

The term pro bono is derived from the Latin phrase 'pro bono publico', meaning 'in the public good'. For centuries lawyers have provided such services.[1]

The Poor Man's Lawyer service

The Poor Man's Lawyer service, which developed in the late 19th century, was an example of a system of organised pro bono help which provided the impetus for social reformers to demand that the state legislate to provide legal aid services to the poor.

The service grew out of the settlement movement which was inspired by the work of Samuel Barnett, a clergyman working in the impoverished East End of London. In the 1880s Barnett formulated a radical proposal to bridge, practically and ideologically, the gap

---

1 See Steve Hynes and Jon Robins, *The justice gap – whatever happened to legal aid?* LAG, 2009 pp7–9.

between rich and poor by building a boarding house for privileged university graduates in one of the most deprived parts of the East End of London. Modelled on the colleges of Oxford with 'sets' of rooms for the students – library, lecture theatre and various function rooms – Toynbee Hall opened in 1884 on Commercial Street near Aldgate.[2] Barnett wantcd to create a community which transcended class barriers, with the graduates providing hands-on educational, social and recreational services to the poor in a spirit of practical neighbourliness. The movement also aimed 'to inquire into the conditions of the poor' and 'to consider and [to] advance plans calculated to promote their welfare'.[3]

This social activism dimension to the settlement movement was led by Frank Tillyard. Tillyard founded the first Poor Man's Lawyer service in 1891 at the Mansfield House settlement. Toynbee Hall (1898) and other settlements quickly followed in its wake. Within a few years of Tillyard's pioneering work, the Poor Man's Lawyer was a firmly established charitable service and it was 'common practice for county court judges and police court magistrates to send Poor Persons' to Poor Man's Lawyer meetings for legal advice'.[4]

By the start of the Second World War, the numbers of such services had increased to 55 in London and 70 in the provinces. The most common cases the services dealt with were disputes between landlord and tenant, accident cases involving workers' compensation, as well as matrimonial cases involving maintenance and separation.[5] It was rare, though, for more than advice to be given, because of lack of resources. Frequently only ten minutes of time could be given to clients.[6] Obvious weaknesses were the absence of co-operation between the various providers, which were mainly dependent on the goodwill of volunteer lawyers, and a lack of unified system of funding. This led to a call by the settlement movement in 1902 for state funding for a legal aid system which deserving applicants could

---

2   Toynbee Hall is one of the original settlement houses still operating, promoting and protecting social welfare. For more information see www.toynbeehall.org.uk.

3   Briggs and Macartney, *Toynbee Hall: the first hundred years*, Routledge, 1984 p9.

4   F Gurney-Champion, *Justice and the poor in England*, Routledge & Kegan Paul, 1926 p16.

5   Gurney-Champion, 1926 p25. See also Leat, 'The rise and role of the Poor Man's Lawyer' (1975) Vol 2 *British Journal of Law and Society* No 2 pp166–181 at p173 – Leat is reporting from a survey of Toynbee Hall's Poor Man's Lawyer in 1901, Gurney-Champion some 25 years later reports very similar concerns.

6   Gurney-Champion, 1926 p20.

access by passing a merits test before a public committee. Toynbee Hall set up its own very limited fund to litigate cases and in 1905 it took 23 cases, the most the scheme ever dealt with. The movement felt a 'growing sense of inadequacy' coping with the demands made upon it.[7]

The 'Poor Man's Lawyer' became a generic name to describe free legal services for the poor and not necessarily associated with the settlement movement. Political parties might organise a service[8] and those provided by local law societies, under what were called the Poor Persons' Rules, were often referred to as Poor Man's Lawyer services. For example, the Manchester Poor Man's Lawyer scheme was run by the local law society and appears to have been the largest service outside London, co-ordinating the work of around 70 firms. At its peak in 1939, these firms advised in 4,290 cases.[9] Coverage was erratic. Towns such as Cardiff and Coventry had no schemes, and some towns would deal with far fewer cases than the better served areas like Manchester.[10] For example, the Newcastle scheme dealt with only 198 cases in 1938.

For over 50 years, despite inadequate geographical coverage and limited resources, the Poor Man's Lawyer services remained the only source of legal advice for many people. By the beginning of the 20th century it was becoming apparent that these services could not meet the demand for legal advice. FCG Gurney-Champion, one of the founders of the movement, recognised the limitations of charity in providing access to justice, saying it made the rule of law 'an anaemic attenuated make-believe which we flourish in the eyes of the poor as "justice"'.[11]

The extent of the movement's influence on the eventual establishment of the legal aid system is difficult to assess. Its legacy, though, is easy to spot in the not-for-profit sector – for example, in the work of the Mary Ward Legal Centre – as well as an inspiration in the creation of the law centre movement in the early 1970s. As vital as these early initiatives were, it should be acknowledged that their help went only so far and few cases were progressed beyond initial advice stopping short of representation in the courts.

7 Gurney-Champion, 1926 p23; Leat, 1975 p176.
8 Letter from Hector Alfred Munro to the Finlay Committee Report on Legal Aid 1926–1928.
9 Robert Egerton, *Legal aid*, The International Library of Sociology and Social Reconstruction, Kegan Paul, Trench, Trubner and Co Ltd, 1945 p147.
10 Ibid p147.
11 Gurney-Champion, 1926 p21.

Pro bono work today

Law firms, barristers, the voluntary sector and law schools carry on the pro bono tradition. There is a strong sense of altruism and professional duty that motivates many lawyers to undertake this work. It also helps many at the beginning of their careers gain experience and, of course, it is has a great public relations value. A substantial amount of work is undertaken on a pro bono basis. A survey of 1,001 solicitors firms conducted by the Law Society in 2007 found that 51 per cent participated in pro bono work. Based on the survey, the Law Society estimated that the equivalent of £338 million – 2 per cent of the total fee income for the firms participating in pro bono work – was given (although there is no breakdown as to what that value constitutes in terms of work).[12]

However, as many commentators have recognised – from LAG to the pioneer of the Poor Man's Lawyer movement Gurney-Champion – pro bono work cannot be a substitute for a properly-funded state system of legal aid. It is a point that today's growing pro bono movement is keen to stress. The influential charity LawWorks, which organises pro bono rotas of solicitors in voluntary organisations and promotes pro bono in the UK, specifies in its protocol: 'Pro bono legal work is always only an adjunct to, and not a substitute for, a proper system of publicly funded legal services'.[13]

In very recent years, pro bono has been elevated from its informal professional pastime status to a significant source of legal help. The London office of Clifford Chance (the world's biggest law firm) was reported to have written off nearly £10 million of work recorded to pro bono files in 2006/07.

Pro bono has been embraced by the political establishment. In 2002 the then Attorney-General, Lord Goldsmith QC (who himself set up a free advice centre in East London's Bethnal Green) set up a pro bono committee, which included the solicitor general Harriet Harman who was to become deputy leader of the Labour party. Harman started her career as an adviser at Brent Law Centre.

Under the present coalition government, the Attorney-General's pro bono committee has continued. The committee plays an important role in organising the National Pro Bono Week, which has been

---

12   Neil Rose, 'Solicitors pro bono work worth £338m', *Law Society Gazette*, 8 November 2007.

13   This has now been subsumed into the *Joint protocol for pro bono work* which covers all branches of the legal profession – see www.probonouk.net/index. php?id=search_results&searchID=protocol&searchsubmit=Go.

running for over ten years now. The week celebrates and promotes the pro bono work of lawyers. According to LawWorks, over 36,500 pieces of pro bono work were undertaken in 2010/11.[14]

Pro bono and divorce law

In forma pauperis

A pro bono system established by Henry VII in 1495 – in forma pauperis – still survived at the beginning of 20th century in much the same form – that is, voluntary help from lawyers on an ad hoc basis. However, it was little used because of a stringent means test and the strong social stigma attached to characterising oneself as 'a pauper' necessary to access the scheme.[15] In 1909 only 66 divorce petitions were filed using the procedure.[16]

It was the rising demand for divorce, which led to further clamour for the reform of the legal services available to the poor.[17] Some 50 years after judicial divorce was introduced in 1857, it remained only available in the High Court in London and was prohibitively expensive costing on average £45 per case (more if witnesses had to be brought from outside London). This was at a time when the average manual wage was £50 per year and, even to get help under the pauperis procedure, a sum of £10 had to be found for solicitors' out-of-pocket expenses.[18]

The Poor Persons Procedure

The pauperis procedural rules were revised by the High Court Rule Committee and renamed the Poor Persons Procedure. When the updated rules were introduced in 1914 a department was created in the Royal Courts of Justice on the Strand in central London to administer the scheme, sift claims and allocate the cases to volunteer solicitors who staffed the scheme. A combination of social change and the upheaval caused by the First World War led to an even greater

---

14 *Pro bono year book 2011* – see www.probonouk.net – p30.
15 Report of the Royal Commission on Divorce and Matrimonial Causes 1912, Cd 6478 ('Gorrell Commission report').
16 Gorrell Commission report, para 69.
17 Tamara Goriely, *Civil legal aid in England and Wales 1914 to 1961: the emergence of a paid scheme*, Doctorate thesis, 2003.
18 Gorrell Commission report, para 69.

demand for divorces. Many people did not want to live with the social stigma of 'living in sin' or illegitimate children. Officials were taken aback by the numbers of applications for help under the revised scheme – in the first week alone of the rules being publicised, over 1,000 applications were received.[19] The previous year had seen only 577 divorce decrees in total.[20]

The Lawrence reports

Increased demand and too few solicitors willing to undertake pro bono work led to the government deciding to form a committee headed by a judge, Mr Justice Lawrence, to report on the demand for and availability of legal services to the poor. This was the first in a long line of committees or reviews established by successive governments to examine legal aid.

Lawrence reported in 1919 and concluded that the Poor Persons' Rules had generally worked well for non-matrimonial cases, but that they failed people seeking help with divorce proceedings. Out of 2,215 applications in 1918, only half were granted petitions, and of these less than half went to trial. The main reason for that was the £10 out-of-pocket expense for the solicitors to proceed with cases.[21] Perversely, Lawrence did not seek to make the system more accessible by reducing the cost. Instead the final recommendations of the committee focussed on reducing demand for the service by recommending a more stringent means test and trying to prevent unscrupulous solicitors profiting from the scheme.

Despite the recommendations being implemented, the new scheme was in crisis by December 1920 because of the demand for divorce from people who had no other way to pay. Still not enough solicitors were willing to provide the service and this prompted a second committee to be set up and, again, chaired by Lawrence.

Reporting in February 1925, the second Lawrence Committee confirmed that the system was failing mainly owing to the unwillingness of solicitors to undertake the work. It was sympathetic to solicitors who were reluctant to carry out the work because of its 'distasteful character'.[22] Alternatives were considered to pay for a service (such

19 Report of the Prescribed Officers in connection with the Poor Persons' Procedure, 1915 (J153/1).
20 L Stone, *Road to divorce: England 1530–1987*, Clarendon, 1990 at p435.
21 Report of Committee to Enquire into the Poor Persons' Rules, 1919, Cmd 430, para 9.
22 Poor Persons' Rules Committee Report, 1925, Cmd 2358.

as a state funding or a levy on the profession) but the committee felt that the voluntary scheme should continue. The committee said:

> [In] our opinion, there exists a moral obligation on the part of the profession, in return for the monopoly in the practice of the law which it enjoys, to render gratuitous legal assistance to those members of the community who cannot afford to pay for such assistance, provided that no undue burden is thereby cast upon any individual members of the profession. The evidence given before us shows that this moral obligation is fully recognised.[23]

It is an interesting comment and reveals a shift from pro bono as an expression of chivalrous or Christian charitable motives to one of professional responsibility. The profession's obligation to undertake pro bono services was expressed as a quid pro quo for its professional monopoly.[24] The committee recommended variously that the administration of the scheme should be transferred from the Poor Persons department in the Royal Courts of Justice to the Law Society, and that the state should pay a grant to support the administrative costs and that the courts in assize towns (those eight towns where High Court judges would sit) should be able to hear cases. This was a boost to the status of the Law Society and to solicitors in general. However, there was an undercurrent in the Lawrence report that reflects the professional rivalry between the Bar and solicitors.

Lawrence did not recommend extending the jurisdiction of the county court to hear divorce cases where solicitors had rights of audience. Jurisdiction remained in the High Court, albeit with some decentralisation of powers to the registries and the eight assize towns.[25] As a consequence, barristers kept their monopoly on advocacy in divorce cases and many were prevented from divorcing because of the prohibitive costs and inconvenience of having to go to London or one of the assize towns. That limitation on jurisdiction was a source of great discontent among people seeking divorce and solicitors alike.

The Finlay Committee

In April 1925 the Lord Chancellor, Viscount Cave, and the Home Secretary, Sir William Johnston-Hicks, appointed the committee on legal aid to the poor to look into 'what facilities exist for giving to

---

23   Poor Persons' Rules Committee Report, 1925 para 12.
24   Goriely (fn 17 above) p76.
25   Poor Persons' Rules Committee Report, 1925 p10.

Poor Persons' advice with respect to their legal rights and liabilities, and aid in the conduct of legal proceedings whether civil or criminal ... and to report what, if any, further steps should be taken in respect of these matters'.[26] The committee was chaired by the judge Mr Justice Finlay.

Divorce and other proceedings in the High Court were excluded from the committee's remit, as these were already within the scope of the existing Poor Persons Procedure. There was disagreement over this as well as other issues in the final committee report. This led to a further dissenting report by two members of the committee in which they called for the extension of the Poor Persons' Rules to the county courts.[27]

Two official reports were published. The first on criminal legal aid was published in March 1926 and was supported by all the committee members. It recommended that the requirement for defendants to disclose their defence in advance should be scrapped and that in limited circumstances magistrates should be given the power to grant legal aid. This led to the Poor Persons Defence Act 1930. A second official report was published in 1928 along with the dissenting report.

Both reports recognised that the social legislation that had been introduced by the government prior to the First World War had increased the need for civil legal advice. Bills introducing health insurance, education, unemployment benefit, pensions, as well as support for the sick and infirm had been passed by the Liberal government in the period 1906–1914. The bills had been supported in parliament by the Liberal Party and the then fledgling Labour Party.

Political attitudes were changing towards the role of the state. In 1909 the then Chancellor of the Exchequer, Lloyd George, had introduced a budget that for the first time had sought to redistribute wealth. The attempt by the House of Lords to reject the budget led eventually to the Parliament Act 1911, which redefined the powers of the Lords. Such reforms were largely a response to social change, most significantly the enfranchising of the working class. Expectations regarding the state's involvement in the provision of services were changing.

The committee heard evidence from, among others, a Miss EA Berthen, a solicitor who had founded two Poor Man's Lawyer services. Berthen argued that without access to a lawyer, people were in danger of feeling powerless and this could lead to discontent and

---

26 Warrant of appointment to the Finlay Committee, 7 April 1925.
27 Minority report para 5.

the disintegration of society. She proposed that Poor Man's Lawyer services should be available to all and, to prevent profiteering by unscrupulous solicitors, that lawyers should be debarred from taking fees in such cases.[28]

In the official report the committee paid a fulsome tribute to lawyers like Berthen who were providing the pro bono services. It appealed to the Law Society and the Bar to establish services where none existed, but it did not see the need of devoting public funds to the work. In responding to a witness who had used the analogy of health to argue for a 'Legal Hospital System' the committee argued that while it was in the state's interests for people to be healthy it was not necessarily in its interest for them to be litigious.[29]

The dissenting report published by two members of the committee was more radical. It argued that the need for advice could not be met by a voluntary service as, because of the expansion of social legislation, there would be a concurrent increase in the numbers of poor people seeking advice. They suggested that lawyers should be employed by local councils to give advice. The service would be paid for from local taxes or the Exchequer, as was the case with the Medical Officer for Health.[30]

Welsh revolt and the collapse of the Poor Persons' Rules

The Finlay Committee failed to recognise that the voluntary scheme was inadequate to meet the burgeoning demand for legal advice. In the years before the Second World War, the Poor Persons scheme collapsed under the weight of this demand, and the independent Poor Man's Lawyer services continued only to meet a fraction of the need for non-family civil legal advice.

Solicitors were divided on whether a voluntary service under the Poor Persons Procedure, administered by the Law Society, should continue. Solicitors in London dominated the Law Society and they rejected a suggestion by the government that solicitors should be paid a set fee for divorce cases for poor people, as they believed it would be 'undignified to convert what had been instituted as charity into a poorly paid business'.[31] Provincial Law Societies thought

28 Letter from EA Berthan to the committee.
29 See para 17.
30 Minority report of Dorothy Jewson and Rhys J Davies.
31 Meeting of the Poor Persons' Rules Committee, 21 October 1938, Law Society Committee Minutes, vol 11 p72.

otherwise. Because of the change in divorce law introduced by the Matrimonial Causes Act 1937, which widened the grounds on which divorce could be granted, demand was far outstripping the supply of pro bono services. Solicitors continued to be unhappy about the restriction of divorce hearings to the High Court as it was less accessible and excluded them from representing clients.

The Law Societies of Wales were especially strident in their opposition to providing services under the Poor Persons Procedure. Their practices were often based in areas where there were high levels of poverty and the numbers of potential clients unable to pay for divorce cases far exceeded the numbers who could. In June 1939, following the lead of the members of the Swansea Law Society who had been striking for a year, the Associated Law Societies of Wales agreed not to undertake any further cases until reasonable fees were paid and rules on which courts could hear cases were reformed.

Faced with the hostility of many provincial solicitors and the outright rebellion against the scheme by Welsh solicitors, the government decided that drastic action was called for and they formed a committee. The Permanent Secretary to the Lord Chancellor, Claud Schuster, wrote to Mr Justice Hodson, asking him to chair the committee. In his letter he suggested that, subject to treasury approval, lawyers should be paid for carrying out the work.[32] Thus it can be argued that the idea for a state-funded legal aid service did not originate with the Law Society, which eventually administered the scheme, but with the government. Hodson's committee never sat, as history intervened.

Citizens Advice

Beginnings

From September 1939 Britain was at war with Nazi Germany and the Axis powers. Wartime conditions led to recognition that the armed forces and civilian population needed access to advice on a range of civil problems. To meet this demand, Citizens Advice Bureaux and voluntary legal advice sessions within the armed services were established. By the end of 1942, a legal aid scheme for armed services personnel had been organised. The Law Society established a salaried solicitor service called the 'Service Divorce Department'. It dealt

---

32   Schuster to Hobson, 15 May 1939 (LCO2 1837) quoted by Goriely (fn 17 above).

with divorce cases for service personnel in the lower ranks for a fee of three guineas paid for by the government. With many solicitors serving in the armed forces and therefore unable to provide pro bono services, the Law Society was forced to drop its objections to a paid service. By the beginning of 1944 it employed five solicitors out of a staff of about 60 including a section dealing with civilian cases.[33]

Over the centuries, pro bono advice services have had lawyers at their core, undertaking legal advice services as part of their professional duty, though as we have seen, some have been more willing than others to do so. In the years before the Second World War, the idea that the public needed advice and other services to assist them with problems began to take shape.

Edward Vivian Birchall died in 1916 at the battle of the Somme in the First World War. He left a note to his friend SP Grundy which said: 'If I am scuppered I'm leaving you £1000 to do some of the things we talked about.' Grundy used this legacy to form the National Association of Guilds of Help which became the National Council for Social Services (NCSS) and later the National Council for Voluntary Services. The purpose of the NCSS was to act as the co-ordinating body for voluntary social work.

In the economic depression of the 1930s it established voluntary schemes for the unemployed, with the support of government funds, as well as encouraging community development in both rural and urban communities. Some local organisations affiliated to the NCSS experimented with free information services for the public. During the Munich crisis in 1938 the first children were evacuated from the towns and cities it became apparent to the NCSS that people would need advice and assistance on problems to do with war-time conditions. A meeting was called which led to plans to establish a network of advice centres to disseminate free, unbiased advice and information.[34]

It was decided that the new service would be called Citizens Advice Bureaux and that it would be managed by the NCSS. As many local organisations in the NCSS already provided personal services to the public, this meant that when war was declared in September 1939, 200 local Citizens Advice Bureaux were immediately up and running. In July 1939 the NCSS had issued a statement on establishing Citizens Advice Bureaux: 'A Service of Advice and help in Time of War.' The NCSS saw Citizens Advice Bureaux as part of the volun-

33   Robert Egerton, *Legal aid*, 1945.
34   See www.ncvo-vol.org.uk/about/NCVO-from-1919-to-1993.

tary sector's response to the challenges of war-time and their role was to work in partnership with both central and national government. The guiding principles underpinning the new service were that each bureau should be organised 'by a community for a community', be run by a committee representing local interests and be open to all. In these original founding statements there is no mention of the now cornerstone principles of the service – free, independent, impartial and confidential.

NCSS used its regional network to persuade local communities to establish further Citizens Advice Bureaux. Local voluntary organisations including churches and clubs would come together, often supported by a local authority, to open a CAB service.[35] Bureaux might be established in a fairly casual way – for example, a London solicitor unable to undertake military service as he had lost an eye, returned from work to tell his wife they were going to set up a CAB in their front room. To assist them in this enterprise he had the Citizens Advice Notes (CANS) produced by NCSS and a box of government leaflets.[36] Through a combination of voluntary effort such as this and grafting Citizens Advice Bureaux services onto existing local NCSS-affiliated organisations, the numbers of advice centres grew rapidly and by January 1940, 1,044 had been launched. While the importance of voluntary effort at a local level cannot be underestimated in initiating new Bureaux, from its inception there was a strong centralised administration and direction to the service which persists to this day.

A grant from the Ministry of Health to the NCSS paid for administrative support to the network of Bureaux. This included a rudimentary information system and a structure of regional offices to develop and support new and existing Bureaux. After the first year, an owl logo was adopted to symbolise the service and plans were put in place to grant certificates of recognition to official outlets. Grants of cash were made by the NCSS to individual Bureaux to help defray costs such as premises, office equipment and paid staff, though local services were also reliant, and remain so, on local authorities and other sources of money.

35   See Margaret E Brasnett, *The story of the Citizens Advice Bureaux*, NCSS, 1964.
36   Jean Richards, *Inform, advise and support*, Lutterworth Press, 1989.

Post-war decline

The Citizens Advice Bureaux service's origins are firmly in information giving, but the service evolved to offer more. Wartime conditions meant that there was a need to get information to people about everything from reserved occupations and exemption from military service, to assisting people in tracing relatives who might be prisoners of war. Bureaux were used by the government as a conduit for spreading information. For example, in July 1941 the rationing of clothes was introduced and the government briefed Bureaux on this prior to its launch in order to ensure that they could advise the public on these new regulations.

Through the war years the types of problems Bureaux dealt with expanded from information on wartime-specific problems, to more generic civil legal problems. By early spring 1940, for example, the Citizens Advice Bureaux in the North West were reporting a 32 per cent increase in problems relating to 'domestic difficulties'. As discussed above, changes in the law and the strain put on relationships owing to wartime conditions led to an increase in demand for advice on divorce and related legal issues. Problems around the resettlement of the millions of returning men and women who had served in the armed forces occupied Citizens Advice Bureaux in the immediate aftermath of the war, but it was the expansion of the welfare state which was to cause the greatest increase in inquiries in the post-war years.

While the Citizens Advice Bureaux service had been founded mainly to disseminate information to the public to do with wartime conditions, it began to position itself for a post-war role. In April 1944 a meeting was held between the Citizens Advice Bureaux service and the Ministry of Health to discuss the possibility of continuing the service after the war. However, in the immediate post-war period there was a gradual decline in funding for the service with the Ministry of Health reducing its grant from £16,750 in 1945 to £5,035 in 1951/52. The numbers of Bureaux reduced from a wartime peak of 1,074 in 1942 to only 477 in 1953.

In the first half of the 20th century pro bono legal services and non-lawyer advice services, the most significant of which was the Citizens Advice Bureaux service, developed largely through voluntary and charitable effort. This type of big society response was typical of how public services were being provided in the 19th and early 20th centuries. Services – most notably education and health – have similar origins, with churches and mutual help societies, for example, providing the funds and other resources to establish them. What they have in common is that they could not meet the demand for assistance from a population who had increasing expectations of the state to assist them when they needed help.

CHAPTER 2

Legal aid from Rushcliffe to Mackay 1949–1997

Criminal legal aid

This book is mainly concerned with the civil legal aid system, but it is important to understand the criminal legal aid system as it has affected the development of civil legal aid, and contributed to the budget problems that have increasingly dominated the thinking of the system's political masters.

Prior to the establishment of the post war civil and criminal legal aid scheme under the Legal Aid and Advice Act 1949, a limited criminal legal aid scheme had existed, to permit the representation of defendants in the higher criminal courts. Under the Poor Prisoners' Defence Act 1903, legal aid was paid if it was deemed that a prisoner had a defence. The Criminal Appeal Act 1907 extended the availability of legal aid to all murder appeals and some other criminal appeals. While few cases were funded under these Acts, they did at least establish the principle that the state should pay for the defence of people accused of a serious crime.

In 1930 a new Poor Prisoners Defence Act extended the 1907 scheme to the police courts or magistrate's courts, as they are now known (also advance disclosure of defence was made no longer compulsory). Legal aid was paid from local funds. Any person who was committed to trial for an indictable offence could apply for a defence certificate if they did not have the means to pay for their legal representation.

Practice on the ground, though, differed widely and was more limited than the generous wording of the statute promised. While the scheme covered all criminal courts, it was not a comprehensive one. People accused of a crime, in a system known as dock briefs, 19 often had to rely on pro bono help from barristers to defend their cases. Prisoners were not usually represented, especially in the lower courts. In 1938 the police courts, which dealt with the majority of offences, sent 19,079 people to prison. Of that number, only 327 had benefited from representation paid through legal aid certificates.[1]

Legal aid for much of the first 25 years of the scheme's existence was mainly a funding system for civil cases, the majority of which were divorce cases. Fifty years ago, in 1962/63, out of a total of £3,639,048 of expenditure on legal aid only £205,324 was spent on criminal cases[2] (this does not, though, include expenditure in the higher courts). Expenditure on criminal legal aid began to grow as it became the norm to have representation in cases before the magistrates' court and in higher court cases. The introduction of the Police and Criminal Evidence Act 1984 which led to representation being available in the police station was another factor this increased expenditure.

From £666 million in 1994, expenditure on criminal legal aid increased to £892 million by 1998. Much of the explanation for this is in the spiralling costs of Crown and higher courts work. Currently, out of a total budget of £1.1 billion for the Criminal Defence Service, £702,892 is spent on Crown and higher court cases.[3] Because of the European Convention on Human Rights, successive governments have been – rightly in LAG's view – reluctant to remove areas of law from the scope of criminal legal aid. They have instead sought to control the budget by squeezing lawyers' fees and other costs.[4]

Throughout the past fifty years, the criminal legal aid budget has expanded on a demand led basis. Around a third of the total budget of £2.1 billion for legal aid is spent on Crown and other higher courts criminal cases. In 2010/11 these cases made up just under 5 per cent of the total number of 2.7 million cases funded by the legal aid system. The last government planned to introduce competitive tendering as a means of controlling the cost of criminal legal aid, but abandoned this policy in July 2009[5] and instead opted for a cut in fees for crown and higher courts work. The current coalition government initially announced that they were going to pursue plans to

1   Robert Egerton, *Legal aid*, 1945 p85.
2   See *Legal aid and advice 1966–67 Report*, Lord Chancellor's Office, p32.
3   Legal Services Commission *Annual report and accounts 2010–11* p9.
4   See Steve Hynes and Jon Robins, *The justice gap – whatever happened to legal aid?* LAG, 2009 pp107–128.
5   V Ling and S Pugh (eds) *Legal aid handbook 2011/12*, LAG p320.

competitively tender for criminal work, but has now delayed these until the autumn 2014.[6]

Legal aid and the welfare state

In 1909 the then Chancellor of the Exchequer Lloyd George's people's budget paved the way for the establishment of the state benefits system which introduced old age pensions and sickness benefits. He was influenced by the example of Germany which had, under Chancellor Bismarck, begun to develop a system of social insurance in the 1880s. The term 'welfare state' seems to have originated in Germany in the 1920s and passed into common usage in the UK and Europe in the 1950s.[7] States had developed social insurance systems in response to the demand from their newly democratically enfranchised populations to tackle social problems such as poverty in old age and unemployment. In Germany the movement to introduce social insurance was partly a response to this, but Bismarck's main reason for adopting the social insurance model was as a political ploy to divide the main opposition to his government which came from the Social Democratic Workers' movement.[8]

It is a persistent misconception in the story of the founding of the legal aid system that it was planned as part of the welfare state, a sort of National Health Service (NHS) for law. Such is the strength of this myth that the Legal Services Commission (LSC), in celebrating the 60th anniversary of the establishment of the system in July 2009, referred to it as the 'fourth pillar' of the welfare state.[9] As the founder of what we now call the welfare state, William Beveridge had talked of four pillars, none of which included law – the LSC got its history wrong.

In his 1942 report 'Social insurance and allied services', Beveridge had called on the state to fight the five 'giant evils': want, disease, ignorance, squalor and idleness; access to justice or lack of it does not get a mention. He was strongly influenced by the experience of the economic depression in the 1930s which had impoverished many people and was a contributing factor to the rise of fascism in Europe.

6 Catherine Baksi 'Ken Clarke postpones legal aid reforms and tendering', *Law Society Gazette*, 1 December 2011 p1.

7 Peter Townsend lecture to the Fabian Society, May 2009.

8 *The Emergence of the Welfare State in Britain and Germany, 1850–1950*, German Historical Institute London, 1981 pp133–134.

9 See: www.legalservices.gov.uk/aboutus/press_releases_10031.asp.

From the 19th century in both education and health a mixed bag of voluntary and local government services had evolved in the UK[10] which Beveridge had studied, leading to him to advocate the establishment of the four pillars of the welfare state:

- the NHS;
- universal housing;
- state security (benefits);
- universal education.

These four pillars led to a flurry of legislation in the post-war period which provided a framework of laws to make Beveridge's vision a reality, providing for the needs of citizens 'from cradle to grave'. These included:

- Education Act 1944;
- Disabled Persons (Employment) Act 1944;
- Family Allowances Act 1945;
- Furnished Houses (Rent Control) Act 1946;
- National Insurance Act 1946;
- National Health Service Act 1946;
- National Insurance (Industrial Injuries) Act 1946;
- National Assistance Act 1948;
- Children Act 1948.

This legislation created a system of state services, but while the legal aid system was established in 1949 it did not at the outset assist the public in enforcing the rights granted to them by the welfare state. This was a role which it evolved to fill over the next thirty years. At its outset, the civil legal aid system mainly met the demand for help with divorce cases, as the pro bono system of advice described in the previous chapter had been overwhelmed by demand in a changing world. It also suited a large section of vested interests in the legal profession.

The Rushcliffe Report

Lord Rushcliffe, a barrister and former Conservative MP, had been given the task of forming a committee to look into establishing a legal aid system in 1944. *A strategy for justice*, published in 1992 by LAG and written by LAG's former director Roger Smith, argued that Rushcliffe largely accepted what the Law Society had proposed to the

10   Frank Field MP, 'The welfare state – never ending reform', BBC website, 10 March 2011.

committee, which was for a legal aid scheme provided by solicitors in private practice and, where appropriate, barristers. The Law Society was concerned to wind up the salaried service Divorce Department (this had been established in the Second World War to assist men and women to obtain divorces), believing the department 'presented too much of a threat for practitioners'.[11] It was also keen for solicitors to re-establish their practices in the aftermath of the war[12] and saw the legal aid scheme as a way to support this.

Suggestions for a salaried service to tackle the housing, debt and benefit problems poorer communities faced were put forward to Rushcliffe by some in the Poor Man's Lawyer and settlement movement[13] (the Haldane Society, for example, argued that the Citizens Advice Bureaux system could form the basis of a salaried lawyer legal aid system), but it was the Law Society's private practice model to meet the demand for assistance with divorce cases which found favour.

Rushcliffe's final report's main recommendations were as follows:

1) Legal aid should be available in those types of cases in which lawyers normally represented private individual clients.
2) Legal aid should not be limited to those people 'normally classed as poor' but should include those of 'small or moderate means'.
3) There should be an increasing scale of contributions payable by those with income or capital above minimum levels, below which legal aid would be free.
4) In addition to a financial means test, cases should be subject to a test of merit, designed to be judged by legal practitioners independent of government, on a similar basis to those applied to private clients.
5) Legal aid should be funded by the state but administered by the Law Society. The Lord Chancellor should be the minister responsible, assisted by an advisory committee.
6) 'Adequate' remuneration should be paid to barristers and solicitors working under the scheme.

11 *The future of publicly funded legal services*, Law Society, February 2003 p34.
12 *The future of publicly funded legal services*, Law Society, February 2003.
13 The submissions from Cambridge House and the Mary Ward Centre argued for this.

The foundation period

While these recommendations were ambitious in their vision and were reflected in the Legal Aid and Advice Act 1949, they were not matched by the reality of what was created in the immediate post-war years. Commentators such as Roger Smith and Joshua Rozenberg[14] refer to the era from 1950, when the scheme was introduced, to 1970 as the 'foundation period'. The legal aid system in these years was restricted in its scope – for example, a survey of certificated cases in Birmingham in 1969 found that 86 per cent of them were for family matters.[15] Criminal legal aid expenditure increased in this period, especially after the Widgery Report[16] in 1966, which had led to legal aid beginning to become the norm for people accused of crimes before the magistrates' courts.

At first, 80 per cent of the population were entitled to civil legal aid on the means test, but successive governments tended to adjust eligibility downwards, so that by 1973 eligibility had collapsed to 40 per cent of the population. Additionally, successive governments tended to take legal issues out of scope of legal aid and to reduce the rates paid to lawyers. These measures were all aimed at controlling expenditure. By 1969/70, £6 million was being spent on civil legal aid and the same sum was being spent on criminal legal aid in the lower courts (higher court criminal continued to be paid separately until 1998). In its 20th annual report (1969/70) on the scheme, the Law Society acknowledged the shortcomings of legal aid, arguing that an advisory service should be added to the scheme as the original act had intended (this had not been implemented because of 'economic problems'[17]). The report also noted that the government did not intend to extend legal aid to the new industrial tribunals and called for the government to look at 'some form of ancillary legal services, of persons with some legal and sociological training'[18] to support clients in the tribunal system.

14   Joshua Rozenberg, *The search for justice*, Hodder & Stoughton, 1994.
15   L Bridges, B Sufrin, J Whetton and R White, *Legal services in Birmingham*, Birmingham University, 1975.
16   *Report of the Departmental Committee on Legal Aid in Criminal Proceedings*, HMSO, 1966.
17   *Legal aid and advice – Report of the Law Society and the comments and recommendations of the Lord Chancellor's Advisory Committee 1969–70* p3.
18   *Legal aid and advice – Report of the Law Society and the comments and recommendations of the Lord Chancellor's Advisory Committee 1969–70* p41.

In the foundation period, the development of legal aid was curtailed for many of the same reasons it faces today. In the early years, the government could fairly blame economic difficulties for its decision not to increase the budget, as victory in the war had come at a high economic price. However, for most of the 1950s and 1960s Britain experienced a post-war economic boom which lasted until the early 1970s. Legal aid's main problem was that it did not enjoy the same political priority as Beveridge's four pillars of the welfare state, in particular health and education, although in the late 1960s political forces pushed legal aid up the government's agenda.

It was increasingly recognised that legal aid was failing impoverished communities and this led to the publication of two influential papers from the Labour and Conservative parties which criticised the lack of access to justice for the public – *Justice for all* by the Society of Labour Lawyers in 1968 and *Rough justice* published by the Conservative Party. *Rough justice* argued that the legal system had to reach out to the poor in order to remedy 'the failure of many people who need legal advice to ever get to a solicitor's office'. Legal academics and activists at the time were also influenced by the setting up in the 1960s of 'neighbourhood law offices' in the United States as part of the War on Poverty programme. This led to the proposal for the establishment of Law Centres staffed by solicitors.

The same influences that fed the clamour for more accessible legal services to serve the poor were also partly responsible for the growth in the social insurance schemes for sickness, unemployment and accidents in the UK. Compared to the rest of Northern Europe, the UK's welfare state has tended to be less generous. Throughout the late 1960s into the 1970s this gap closed, though it opened up again from the mid-1970s onwards.[19] The increase in scope of the legal aid system in this period can be seen as part of a general expansion of the welfare state and a response to a population with a less deferential view of public services – if people were refused a benefit or a service they were more likely to want to take advice rather than simply accept a decision.

---

19 Daniel Wincott, 'Images of welfare law and society: the British welfare state in comparative perspective', *Journal of Law and Society*, September 2011.

Legal aid's golden period?

If there was a golden age in the history of legal aid during which Rushcliffe's founding principles looked as if they might be adhered to, it is the period from 1973 to 1986. As well as coinciding with the parallel development of the voluntary sector advice services (see next chapter), the period kicked off in 1973 with the establishment of the advice and assistance, or 'green form' scheme as it became known, and ended with the implementation of the Police and Criminal Evidence Act 1984 (PACE) in 1986. This was the last large expansion of the legal aid scheme and it led to the establishment of the right to legal advice for anyone detained in a police station – an important safeguard against miscarriages of justice as in the UK's adversarial system where the trial very much starts at the police station.

Duty schemes in the magistrates' courts were given a statutory basis in 1984. These, combined with the duty schemes established in police stations, set the pattern for the provision for criminal law services which remain to the present day. The expansion of criminal and family legal aid helped pay for the growth in firms, and by 1986 legal aid represented 11 per cent of solicitors' incomes – up 5 per cent in ten years.

Under the green form scheme, advice on any matter of English law could be given to a client after the application of a simple means test. The scheme had been called for by the Law Society in response to the *Justice for all* and *Rough justice* papers referred to above and to stave off the perceived threat to the private practice model of provision that the Law Centres and other voluntary sector services posed. In 1982 it was expanded to include representation before mental health review tribunals. Prior to losing office in 1979, the Labour government increased the percentage of the population entitled to claim legal aid to 79 per cent – it had been 40 per cent in 1973 at the start of this period.

Despite the introduction of green form legal aid, LAG reported that by 1986 there was only a 10.7 per cent increase in social welfare law cases being undertaken under the scheme. Over half of the million green forms in 1986 were still for the now traditional core areas of legal aid practice – crime and family.[20] There is a structural bias towards this embedded in the system which persists. It largely suited firms to establish civil practices in family law in the foundation period of legal aid as it complemented paying divorce work. As

20   *A strategy for justice*, LAG, 1992 p9.

criminal legal aid work expanded, firms developed businesses linked to referrals from magistrates' courts and police rotas, as well as building up own client work. It should also be stated that increases in the numbers of firms undertaking legal aid work in the late 1970s and early 1980s were caused in part by a recession which led solicitor firms to seek to diversify into other areas of work including legal aid. Conveyancing, which was a mainstay of the traditional high street practice, was also less profitable as legislation passed in 1985 ended the solicitors' monopoly on this, and contributed to a shift to other work.

Legal aid becomes a policy problem

The period of expansion in legal aid came to an abrupt end in March 1986. The figures show that there had been a 50 per cent increase in legal aid expenditure in two years[21] and that the rises were greater than the number of clients served. Cost increases in this period cannot be fully explained by increases in eligibility. In response, the government rushed through legislation in what LAG described at the time as a 'shock move' to cut eligibility to legal aid. *Legal Action* reported in March 1986:

> The backdoor nature of this legislation coupled with the complete absence of consultation, has stunned legal services groups accustomed to a more leisurely pace of action (if not complete inaction) by the Lord Chancellor.[22]

Worse was to come. LAG's annual general meeting in May 1986 discussed the looming crisis in legal aid. The outlook for legal aid was described as 'grim' and its administration by the Law Society was described as a 'disaster area'. Members feared that the review which had been announced by the government would mean cuts in provision, and even the consideration of measures such as fixed fees to reduce expenditure.[23] However, the review only resulted in minor changes to the green form scheme. It had suggested transferring large parts of the green form scheme to the voluntary sector in an updated version of the ideas put to the Rushcliffe Committee and transferring administration of legal aid to an independent body. Both

21 May 1986 *Legal Action* 4.
22 March 1986 *Legal Action* 3.
23 May 1986 *Legal Action* 4.

suggestions which were welcomed by LAG at the time.[24] Both ideas were shelved.

The Citizens Advice Bureaux service rejected the idea of the transfer of legal aid, while welcoming the review's recognition of the role of the voluntary sector in legal services. Director Elizabeth Filkin, while personally thought to favour the proposal to shift green form to the Citizens Advice Bureaux service, told LAG 'we will not be party to any attempt at cost cutting or reducing legal services to the poor'.[25] A major stumbling block for the Citizens Advice Bureaux service in considering taking on green form work was that it would undermine its principle of free access as clients would need to be means-tested to qualify.

It was from the mid-1980s that the perception grew among policy makers that legal aid expenditure was a problem to be dealt with. With their re-election in 1987, the Conservatives returned to the battleground of legal aid reform. In a surprise move by then Prime Minister Margaret Thatcher, Lord Mackay was appointed Lord Chancellor and continued in office until the Conservatives' loss of power to Labour in 1997. Mackay was from outside the London-based legal establishment, being a Scottish lawyer with working-class roots.

The Legal Aid Act 1988

The Legal Aid Board

Lord Mackay picked up responsibility for a bill to reform legal aid from his predecessor and piloted the Legal Aid Act 1988 through the legislative process. LAG was disappointed with the bill, as it gave no statement of purpose about what legal aid was for, but merely saw it as an administrative problem to be solved. The centrepiece of the legislation was the replacement of the Law Society with the Legal Aid Board (LAB) as administrators of the scheme, a move which LAG saw as 'uncontroversial'.[26] With the changeover to a government 'quango' (non-departmental public body, to use the correct term) with its own governing board, control of legal aid policy had been snatched from the lawyers. The establishment of the Legal Aid Board ushered in a new era for legal aid in which the government showed little concern

---

24   July 1986 *Legal Action* 2.
25   December 2006 *Legal Action* 6.
26   January 1988 *Legal Action* 6.

for legal aid policy and was largely content for the Legal Aid Board to get on and run the system.

Half of the new board were drawn from business. LAG recognised that the administrative shortcomings of the Law Society run system needed to be addressed, but expressed concern about reductions in eligibility, as well as the disproportionate amount of expenditure going on crime and family cases while neglecting other work. LAG also had concerns about the viability of fee levels[27] – the Act abolished the old calculation of legal aid fees which had been based on a discounted market rate and gave the Lord Chancellor sole responsibility for setting rates.

Steve Orchard was appointed as the first chief executive of the Legal Aid Board in December 1988. He had worked his way up the civil service career ladder in the Courts Service where he started as a clerk at the age of 17 in Poole County Court. His appointment confirmed the view that the Lord Chancellor had wanted a competent manager to oversee the Legal Aid Board rather than a lawyer with direct experience of legal services. Orchard's appointment proved crucial as he, along with the board, came to dominate legal aid policy, leading Roger Smith to comment in 1997:

> The Board's command of its brief; its business-dominated approach; its possession of the empirical detail of legal aid and its sheer effectiveness have given it a lead role in policy making. Much of this strength flows from the force of character of its chief executive since its beginning, Steve Orchard.[28]

The Legal Aid Board ran legal aid for over ten years to 2000, when the Legal Services Commission (LSC) was formed. Control of expenditure was mainly achieved by changing eligibility and scope in civil legal aid. In 1992/93 the percentage of households eligible for civil legal aid was drastically reduced from 77 per cent to 53 per cent, and in subsequent years nibbled away to levels which made civil legal aid largely a sink service for people on means-tested benefits. Scope was also changed. One of Mackay's first moves was to take probate and property advice out of the green form scheme. The political imperative to control the budget largely at the expense of access to justice in this period meant that the bureaucrat was in the assent over the lawyers who wanted to expand the system.

Steve Orchard described the green form system as 'a problem'. He also believed that costs generally were not being controlled, say-

27 June 1988 *Legal Action* 3.
28 Roger Smith, *Justice: redressing the balance*, LAG, 1997 p33.

ing: 'Many solicitors were milking the system.' The number of green form cases increased by 50 per cent in the ten years to 1997. There were some abuses, which are discussed in chapter 4, but the growth in green form cases can be explained in large part though by the increasing demand for advice. By the end of the 1990s, Citizens Advice Bureaux alone were dealing with over 5.5 million problems. The 1.5 million green form cases therefore need to seen in this context, albeit that many of the problems Citizens Advice Bureaux dealt with might be classified as generalist as opposed to legal ones. Roger Smith outlines the problem succinctly: 'There is a massive need for legal advice and an infinite need for general advice'. At its heart, the green form scheme was a valiant attempt to ensure access to legal advice on any legal problem, but it fell foul of budget constraints and the temptation of some to use it for low-level enquiries to maximise profit.

In the Legal Aid Board period, eligibility and scope were not reduced for criminal legal aid. Orchard says: 'With crime we had to assess and pay the bills for the magistrates' court and police station work. There was no room for any huge policy changes'. The figures throughout the decade to 1998 for the magistrates' court rotas and police station work were stable, reaching £33 million and £82 million respectively, by the end. The introduction of standard fees in magistrates' court representation in 1993/94 had little impact on costs, as they rose much in line with inflation. Orchard's major concern was that in both crime and civil there were too many 'dabblers' in legal aid: 'In London for example 40 per cent of the firms did 90 per cent of the work'.

The Legal Aid Board's main policy initiative under Orchard was the introduction of franchising. It was originally sold to practitioners as a non-compulsory system of quality assurance which would give them higher fees and free them from bureaucratic controls. By April 1997, out of a total of 12,000 legal aid firms a total of 1,740 were franchised. In franchised firms, management audits were carried out against a set of 'good practice' criteria. These included policies on independent file review, conflicts of interests and complaints through to personnel policies such as equal opportunities recruitment, professional development and others. Files were audited against checklists known as transaction criteria. Transaction criteria were supposed to check the quality of work for individual clients, but had only partial success in achieving this. Accreditation schemes for family law and police station work were also introduced in conjunction with the Law Society. In addition to these quality initiatives, the Legal Aid Board ran a pilot project of 42 voluntary advice agencies requiring them to work to franchise standards. This was to have great significance in the next phase of the development of the legal aid system which saw a greater participation of the not-for-profit sector in the scheme and the use of franchising and contracting to concentrate the service amongst fewer specialist suppliers.

CHAPTER 3

The legal rights – chicken and egg

Social welfare law

Social welfare law (SWL) has become the accepted term by many for areas of civil law that impact on poor and disadvantaged communities. Housing, benefits, immigration, debt, employment, community care, education and other areas of public law, may all be included in the definition of SWL. The first four are the biggest areas of spend currently for the civil legal aid scheme, after family law, at the time of writing (October 2012). The following table breaks down the cases and legal aid budget for SWL and are based on LAG's research[1] (see appendix 7 for a summary of the government's original estimates of the planned civil cuts).

	Advice	Cases	Representation	Cases
Debt	£20m	10,5000		50
Education	£0.5m	2,800	£0.5m	70
Employment	£5m	24,000	£0.5m	70
Housing	£10m	52,000	£3m	1,200
Welfare benefits	£25m	135,000		
Immigration	£20m	53,000	£1m	290
Total	*£80.5m*	*277,300*	*£5m*	*1,680*

1 *Revised figures for cuts in social welfare law*, LAG, November 2011.

Benefits, debt, employment and housing are the largest areas of enquiry for the Citizens Advice Bureaux (CABx) service. Benefits and debt, with over 2 million face to face enquiries in Citizens Advice Bureaux for each, are by a large margin the most common reason that a member of the public will visit the Citizens Advice website (see appendix 1). Benefits and tax credits, at over 4 million, also tops the numbers of hits on the Citizens Advice website (see appendix 2). For the public, SWL problems are the most common that they are likely to encounter, but civil legal aid for much of its history did not provide services to advise and represent people with these problems of everyday life.

The expansion of legal aid between 1973 and 1986, discussed in the previous chapter, did lead to a significant increase in private sector practitioners who developed practices including SWL. However, as already argued, they still tended to concentrate on family law. It was mainly in the not-for-profit sector that SWL specialisms developed and eventually became integrated into the civil legal aid system. Rising unemployment, which peaked at 3.5 million in May 1985, along with increases in the numbers of lone parents, an aging population, as well as a growing awareness of rights amongst disadvantaged groups, fed the demand for SWL advice services through the late 1970s and 1980s. This was met for the most part by local government funding of not-for-profit organisations to provide advice services. A key influence in the development of this was the Citizens Advice Bureaux service.

Citizens Advice Bureaux

Going it alone

After shrinking in the immediate post-war period, the revival of the Citizens Advice Bureaux service mainly came about through the national association's recognition of the emerging importance of advice in housing and consumer law. In 1955 it set up a committee to look at the problems associated with hire-purchase agreements, which were increasingly used as a means of purchasing consumer goods. It also published information on housing problems as the public were increasingly seeking advice on these. In recognition of this in 1960, the Ministry of Housing and Local Government made a grant of £2,500 to the national organisation to provide support to Bureaux. The Board of Trade gave a grant in 1963 of £24,000 to support work on consumer advice. These grants gave the movement a sound financial basis, but they were a contributing factor in the split from its parent organisation, the National Council of Social Service (NCSS). Put simply, the Citizens Advice Bureaux department had outgrown NCSS and was ready to go it alone.

It was the consumer movement of the early 1970s that really gave the Citizens Advice Bureaux service the boost to become the national service we know today.[2] In 1973 the government renewed the grant to the National Association of Citizens Advice Bureaux (NACAB), or Citizens Advice as the national organisation is now called. This was an unexpected move by the conservative politician, Sir Geoffrey Howe, who was then Minister for Trade and Consumer Affairs. He was later to serve as Chancellor of the Exchequer in Mrs Thatcher's first government, before becoming Foreign Secretary. In a meeting with the then director of NACAB, Jeremy Leighton, he said he was considering giving the organisation a grant to strengthen the capacity of Bureaux to advise consumers. The new grant was confirmed in December that year and £200,000 was paid the following year. By 1976/77 a grant of £500,000 to promote new Bureaux and to upgrade existing ones was made to the national association.

Citizens Advice now receives around £45 million in government grants and the local Bureaux have an income of £141 million, mainly received from local government. As discussed in the next chapter, the Legal Services Commission (LSC) has become an increasingly important funder and currently has contracts worth £30 million with Citizens Advice Bureaux. The core grant for the national organisation continues to be made by the Department for Business, Innovation and Skills (BIS), the successor of the Department of Trade and Industry, so while this grant's origins are ostensibly to support consumer advice, the services offered by Bureaux are mainly related to debt, including utilities and credit debts, as well as users of the welfare state's benefits system. With employment and housing making-up the two next largest categories of enquiry, it is difficult to escape the conclusion that the Citizens Advice Bureaux service is the largest state supported civil legal advice institution. The reason it has tended mainly to offer advice in these areas of SWL is down to the demand from members of the public who walk through the doors of their local Bureau. Successive governments have been happy to allow the Citizens Advice service to continue in this role and it has become a national institution with the injunction 'if you need advice on this, go to your local CAB' embedded in many official forms from the state.

2 Jean Richards, *Inform, advise and support*, Lutterworth Press, 1989.

A matter of principles

The one time the Citizens Advice Bureaux service faced a major political threat illustrates its strengths as an organisation. The Conservative minister, Sir Gerard Vaughan, threatened to cut the grant to NACAB after he became embroiled with the Citizens Advice Bureaux service in a row over political bias.[3] As Minister of State for Consumer Affairs, he wrote to NACAB in March 1983 stating that he was only authorising a six-month grant to the national association for the year 1984/85. He said he was concerned about the quality of services provided by some bureaux and the efficiency of the national organisation. It seems, though, that his real motive for his intervention was the third reason he gave, which was the alleged political bias of some local bureaux and national association employees. Vaughan's mistaken impression about political bias in the Citizens Advice Bureaux service seems to have been not unrelated to the fact that the organiser at his local bureau in Reading was one Joan Ruddock. At the time, Ruddock enjoyed a high public profile as the Chairman of the Campaign for Nuclear Disarmament (CND).[4] In the early 1980s, CND was at the forefront of the political debate on nuclear weapons after the deployment of American missiles at bases in the UK. The Reading Bureau had gone to 'extreme care' to ensure that Ruddock kept her work separate from her political role,[5] but the minister seemed to believe that left-wing activists were rife in the Citizens Advice Bureaux service.

The minister's attack galvanised the service, at both a national and local level, into a highly effective campaign to defend itself, which emphasised its principles of independence, impartiality and objectivity. Dr Vaughan announced a review of the service to be carried out by management consultants, but he was already on the back foot when he did this, having conceded in a speech to the House of Commons on 12 April that the government had 'full confidence in the Citizens Advice movement'. His earlier remarks on the service had unleashed a storm of protest from MPs of all political parties who had received letters of complaint from their local Bureaux. The media coverage of the affair was also hostile to the government after Martin Kettle at the *Observer* broke the story in a piece sympathetic to NACAB. By the time an adjournment debate took place over the issue in the House

---

3   Sir Gerard Vaughan, 'Obituaries', *Telegraph*, 16 August 2003.
4   'Obituary', *Guardian*, 5 August 2003.
5   *Inform, advise and support* (fn 2 above) p20.

of Commons on 28 May 1984, the minister could be described as having become fully on message, saying:

> Our citizen's advice bureaux are a major national asset ... we have nearly 1,000 serviced by over 10,000 voluntary workers ... The dedication, competence and impartiality of the service are known to all who are in contact with it ... The Bureaux offer free ... and confidential advice to some 4 million enquiries a year.[6]

The Vaughan affair illustrated the strengths of the Citizens Advice Bureaux movement. Its central co-ordinating association, NACAB, has successfully embedded the core principles of the movement across the service. Most significantly, its deep-rooted local support across the country was, and remains, non-party political. What Vaughan had not realised was that many of 10,000 voluntary workers he referred to, and the paid staff in bureaux, were extremely well-connected, often with direct links to their local MPs built by contacts through casework and via civic institutions, including the Conservative Party. In attacking the Citizens Advice Bureaux service he was offending a large part of the establishment, as was remarked upon recently with regard to the political influence the service enjoys, 'because the wives of Tory MPs volunteer for CABs'.[7] He had picked the wrong enemy for the wrong reason. In an incident that occurred while his review of the service was ongoing, he offered a lift to the then director of NACAB, Elizabeth Filkin, and remarked, 'I think you are going to come out of this better than I am'.[8] He was proved right. The review concluded that NACAB, apart from some mild criticisms, was sound, and recommended an increase in its grant. Vaughan was dropped at the next reshuffle and did not hold ministerial office again.

Independent advice centres

The network of advice centres, backed up by an effective national organisation, is what gives the Citizens Advice Bureaux movement its political clout. Above all, the open-door advice and other services it provides are popular with the public and ensure that the Citizens Advice Bureaux brand is credible. However, such is the dominance of the Citizens Advice Bureaux brand it tends to overshadow

6 *Hansard*, 28 May 1984.
7 Fiona Bawdon, 'Advice agencies in crisis: "We will just disappear. No one will notice"', *Guardian*, 3 February 2012.
8 *Inform, advise and support* (fn 2 above) p21.

the equally large network of independent advice centres, many of which were established in the same period of expansion of advice services in the UK. These centres often specialise in areas of SWL and are, like Citizens Advice Bureaux, most frequently paid for by local government. They were often founded by interest groups, such as the Royal Association of Deaf People Law Centre, or to serve a particular ethnic group, such as Welwitschia Legal Advice Centre in the London borough of Haringey, which was established to assist Angolan nationals.

Advice UK

Advice UK was conceived in 1979 as the national organisation for the independent advice centres. A core of around 200 centres decided that they needed a national voice for their sector, in the same way as the Law Centres had done with the Law Centres Federation (discussed below), and Citizens Advice Bureaux had with NACAB. They hoped to secure a government grant to support their work, in the same way as the other two national organisations had been successful in doing. However, according to Steve Johnson, the director of Advice UK, they have never succeeded in doing this as they are not a 'branded franchise' and in the aftermath of the Vaughan affair, 'what civil servant would recommend to a minister redistributing some of the cash which was granted to CAB?' According to Johnson, this has resulted in around '40 per cent of the sector being ignored by government', but he believes independent advice centres embody 'all the virtues of civil society, as they are formed by people who getting together in grass roots initiatives to meet the need for advice in their local communities'.

Johnson argues that not being tied to strict membership rules like Citizens Advice Bureaux, or the regulation of solicitors which Law Centres are, has meant that the independent advice sector is 'more flexible and able to innovate'. He points to the development of debt counselling services by the Advice UK member, Birmingham Settlement, in the late 1970s as an example of an innovation that affected the whole sector. He and others associated with independent advice centres also argue that the client-centred approach that independent centres adopted in the 1970s as being influential on the Citizens Advice Bureaux service. Currently, Advice UK includes in its membership of around 800, large organisations to small community based groups. Advice UK derives some of its income from providing services to its members, including professional indemnity insurance. It also undertakes research and other projects to support advice services. The organisation's recent report[9] on systems thinking has been influential. One of the major findings of the research was that over 40 per cent of the problems which advice centres deal with are caused by failures in decision-making in public authorities. Eliminating these systems failures would free-up capacity in the advice sector, Advice UK argues.[10]

Other services

Many local councils, in addition to the voluntary sector advice services established in the 1970s and 1980s, developed in-house services, mainly in welfare rights. By 1997, 120 local authorities had opened welfare rights services.[11] These new welfare rights and other SWL advice services were often linked to local councils' anti- poverty strategies, an important part of which was to ensure the take-up of benefits and other rights. In recent years, these services have come under pressure from budget cuts as some local councils have moved away from funding them, as they have no legal requirement to do so. Manchester, a Labour controlled council, for example, announced it was closing its advice service, one of the largest in the country last year (2011) to save £1.7 million. It did reprieve some of the service, but still plans to cut much of it.[12]

The Child Poverty Action Group (CPAG) is a national charity which has played a lead role in providing information on benefits and other services to support advice agencies in the not-for-profit sector and directly by local authorities. The charity has taken many test cases on behalf of claimants over the years and has made a huge contribution to the development of the law on welfare benefits. In the field of welfare benefits, many non-legally qualified caseworkers have become adept at identifying points of law to take to a further appeal. Organisations like CPAG, which employs lawyers, can take such cases to the higher courts.

9   *It's the System, Stupid! Radically re-thinking advice*, Advice UK, 2008.

10 *Radically re-thinking advice services in Nottingham*, November 2009, available at: www.adviceuk.org.uk/_uploads/documents/1MicrosoftWord-NottinghamSystemsThinkingPilot-InterimReport.pdf.

11 Neil Bateman, *Practising welfare rights*, Routledge/Community Care, 2006 p21.

12 'Council U-turn as Manchester Advice Service is given reprieve', *Manchester Evening News*, 12 July 2011.

Law Centres

One of the reasons that voluntary and other non-lawyer services have grown in the UK is that the provision of most legal advice to the public is not restricted to lawyers – it should be noted that immigration advice is regulated and non lawyers providing this service need to be accredited.[13] Non-lawyer services have grown in the private sector as well. In many tribunals, a legal qualification is not required to represent clients, and so for example in employment tribunals both lawyer and non-lawyer firms represent employees and employers before the tribunals. Referrals in SWL cases requiring an appeal to a higher court, such as those referred to organisations like CPAG, can work well, but the system can break down if a frontline advice organisation fails to identify that legal remedy is appropriate.

In the county courts and most other courts, rights of audience are required to represent in court and only qualified lawyers are able to conduct litigation on behalf of clients. Non-lawyers can only speak on behalf of litigants at the discretion of the judge. One of the most frequent complaints about non-lawyer advice centres is that they tend to hold onto cases when they should be referring them to a lawyer to pursue a legal solution. An experienced CAB employee told LAG in an interview for this book that when training volunteer and paid advisers in Bureaux, one frequently encountered problem is their tendency to try to act as an arbiter in a case rather than advising a client on a legal solution, even when it is appropriate. Not being able to litigate has meant that Citizens Advice Bureaux and other advice services are often not seen as a threat by local government (their largest funder), but can mean that clients are let down if they are not referred to a service that provides representation in court.

Law Centres, as they employ solicitors, are able to conduct litigation and so can bridge the gap between non-solicitor agencies and private practice. However, Law Centres can litigate against local councils, for example in housing and social care cases, so many local councils have proved hostile to their development. The Law Centre movement's influence on the development of legal services has proved greater than the numbers of such services on the ground.

The first Law Centre was set-up in a former butchers shop premises in North Kensington, London, and opened on 17 July 1970. It was

---

13   See Immigration and Asylum Act 1999 Part V. This restricts the provision of immigration advice to those persons regulated by the Office the Immigration Services Commissioner.

based in a poor, ethnically diverse, inner city area with overcrowded, dilapidated housing and low-paid work. As with the Law Centres that followed it, the Centre was accountable to the community it served through a management committee elected from local people. The founding of the Law Centres movement challenged the legal establishment. The Law Society was initially hostile to the development of Law Centres because solicitors in private practice felt threatened by what amounted to a salaried legal service.

After pressure from a group of solicitors in Hillingdon, West London, protesting against the establishment of a Law Centre in their area in 1975, the Law Society tried to stop solicitors practising in Law Centres. This led to government intervention and an agreement was eventually struck with the Law Society, which allowed the continued existence of Law Centres on the understanding that they would specialise in areas of work that did not impinge on the commercial interests of private practice.

After this agreement, Law Centres mainly developed services in SWL rather along the lines which had been called for by the voluntary services in their contributions to the Rushcliffe Committee. They played an important role in increasing awareness of legal rights, especially in housing. Many solicitors who worked in Law Centres would go on to establish high street practices which still undertake housing and other areas of SWL.

Law Centres have a well established reputation for being at the cutting edge of developments in social welfare law. Examples of leading cases include one in which Camden Law Centre in London represented employees who had been unfairly dismissed but were prevented from bringing a case because they had less than two years' service[14] – this led to a change in the law on unfair dismissal. In a 2006 case, Hammersmith and Fulham Law Centre represented clients who had claimed asylum after coming to the UK from Afghanistan. This case gained some notoriety as the refugees had taken the extreme action of hijacking a plane to get to the UK. The nine Afghan dissidents had been acquitted of hijacking the plane that had brought them to the UK by successfully arguing duress, but the government, from the Prime Minister Tony Blair down, fuelled by tabloid press outrage, was determined to try to circumvent the law and not grant them asylum. It delayed making a decision on their application, attempting to make changes in the law, but this failed

14 *R v Secretary of State for Employment ex p Seymour-Smith and Perez*, C-167/97, [1999] 2 AC 554, 9 February 1999.

after the Law Centre successfully defended the case on behalf of their clients in the Court of Appeal.[15] This case illustrates that Law Centres sometimes have found themselves having to defend the rule of law against political interests.

In the early years, Law Centres did not have reliable finances and were dependent on charitable grants. In 1974, the first grants were made by local government and, the following year, the Lord Chancellor's Department made grants to ensure the future of eight Law Centres. At this point the government was committed to diverting some resources from legal aid to developing a network of Law Centres, but the change of government in 1979 led to a change in this policy.[16] The incoming Conservative government took the view that any further expansion of Law Centres should be funded by local government. Direct grants continued to the eight Law Centres and these were eventually converted to contracts after the expansion of legal aid in the not-for-profit sector which took place under the Labour government of 1997–2010, which is described in the next chapter.

Up until 1982, the Department of the Environment, through its Inner Urban Aid programme, had funded many new Law Centres and other advice centres.[17] After this date, local government was increasingly the major funder of SWL advice. With this support, the number of Law Centres grew from half a dozen in 1974 to a peak of over 60 in the mid-1980s. The Law Centres Federation (LCF) was founded in 1978 to promote the development of more Law Centres. The LCF received a grant from the then Lord Chancellor's Department, which has continued to the present day.

Redution in numbers

The number of Law Centres has always been dwarfed by the number of Citizens Advice Bureaux and other independent advice centres. By 1986 there were 1,236 generalist advice agencies providing advice on benefits and other areas of SWL.[18] There has been some fall back in numbers mainly caused by cutbacks in spending. Currently, there are 55 Law Centres, around 400 main Citizens Advice Bureaux

---

15 (2006) *Times* 5 August.

16 Cyril Glasser, 'LAG's early days: some reflections', October 1997 *Legal Action* 4.

17 Mike Stephens, *Community Law Centres: a critical appraisal*, Ashgate Publishing, 1990 p114.

18 Berthoud, Benson and Williams, *Standing up for claimants*, Policy Studies Institute, 1986.

working out of over 3,000 locations and around 800 independent advice organisations which are members of Advice UK.

The expansion of the not-for-profit sector

The development of advice services in parallel with the legal aid system is an important part of the history of increasing access to civil justice. These services are rooted in the vision of the NCSS, the Citizens Advice Bureaux service and the pioneers of pro bono advice. Expansion was influenced by the failure of the legal aid system and most private practice solicitors to meet the demand for SWL advice from the public. Another important factor was the increase in legislation in SWL. The founding statutes of the welfare state were built on a raft of legislation in social security, housing, employment and other areas of SWL. The public needed advice and information to enforce the rights these, and the continuing stream of new legislation which pours out of parliament, gives them. The rise in mass unemployment in the 1970s and 1980s meant there was a pent-up demand for the take-up of advice about rights to benefits and the other areas of SWL, to which local councils and the advice sector responded.

Without the growth in non-legal aid advice services, it is doubtful whether there would have been the development of SWL services and the increased take-up of rights throughout the 1970s and 1980s. Legal rights in SWL suffer from a chicken and egg syndrome – without the services in place to promote awareness of their existence and to provide advice and representation, the public do not use them. However, as much of SWL advice sector is predominantly paid for by local government there is an uneven distribution of such services, which has contributed to central government downgrading their importance. There are also variations in the quality and type of the services provided. The introduction of legal aid contracts described in the next chapter helped raised standards, but there remain big variations in services. Many Citizens Advice Bureaux and other advice centres do little more than give information on the law, while others will provide casework services in SWL of the same, if not higher standard, than lawyers.

CHAPTER 4

New Labour reforms 1997–2002

In May 1997, after 18 years in power, the Conservatives suffered a devastating defeat to a reinvigorated and rebranded Labour party which swept into office with a majority of 179 seats, the largest they had ever enjoyed. Part of the New Labour message was that it was not wedded to the ideology of the past, though it should be stressed past Labour governments had often had a more pragmatic approach than their political rhetoric might suggest. New Labour made significant breaks with the past in its campaign for election in 1997 which would have important consequences for all areas of policy, including legal aid. Labour decided to stick to the outgoing government's spending limits, and accepted the need for markets to regulate the cost and delivery of public services.

Legal aid under Lord Irvine

The first phase of New Labour's stewardship of legal aid policy was presided over by Lord Derry Irvine, who became Lord Chancellor when Labour came into power. In its manifesto *New Labour: because Britain deserves better*, Labour promised to establish a 'community legal service', introduce better regional planning of services and have a wide ranging review of legal aid. *Legal Action* was critical of both the Conservatives and Labour, stating in an editorial in March 1997:

> Both the government and the Labour opposition have stitched themselves into a corner. In just over two years time, both have committed themselves to making real cuts in expenditure to a program that is rising at ten per cent a year.[1]

1 March 1997 *Legal Action* 3.

LAG in 1997 published the book *Justice: redressing the balance*, which discussed ideas for the reform of legal services. The book was intended to influence the new government's review of civil justice and publicly funded legal services which had been set up under Sir Peter Middleton. It argued that eligibility and scope should be extended as far as possible within the budgetary constraints. Among its suggestions, the book advocated for a soft cap on legal aid expenditure rather than a hard cap which would prevent expenditure over the allocated budget; legal aid being extended to tribunal representation; and that there should be better planning of services.

Interest groups such as LAG were caught on the back foot by the new Lord Chancellor, as he announced radical plans for the reform of legal aid at the Law Society's annual conference in November 1997. In his speech he outlined plans to take most civil legal aid cases out of the legal aid scheme. Family cases would remain in the scheme and he proposed that the bulk of other cases in the future would be funded by conditional fee arrangements. All claims for money or damages would no longer be covered by legal aid. In an attempt to portray this move as widening access to justice to middle class people above the income limits for legal aid, details of the speech had been trailed in the *Mail on Sunday* and the *Times*. Sir Peter Middleton's report on legal aid was published to accompany Lord Irvine's announcements and affirmed that all legal aid money claims could be replaced by conditional fees (ie 'no win no fee' agreements). In his speech, Lord Irvine said:

> Excluding claims for money or damages from legal aid will put those on low income, as well as those on middle or higher incomes, on an equal footing – taking forward a civil case will depend on whether or not it has merit to persuade a lawyer to handle it on a 'no win no fee' basis.

Much of Lord Irvine's policies on legal aid were dictated by the fact that he was not allocated any new money to the legal aid budget. For the entire New Labour period, legal aid policy was dominated by the need to contain the budget, as spending on legal aid was not a priority. At the time, the *Financial Times* described Lord Irvine's proposals for legal aid as 'not so much New Labour but Old Treasury'.[2] Consumer groups opposed it, arguing that because of the cost of insurance premiums, many of the poorest would be excluded or risk having large amounts of their compensation eaten up by success fees. LAG estimated as much as £100 million in compensation would be lost by 75,000 people

2   Philip Stephens, *Financial Times*, 1997.

whose cases were currently funded by legal aid.[3] Personal injury specialists, though, were caught in a cleft stick over the proposals as they had argued for the introduction of conditional fees.[4]

While the extension of 'no win no fee' arrangements grabbed the headlines, Lord Irvine made other announcements in the speech which were to set the direction for the first phase of New Labour policy towards legal aid: contracts with fixed prices for blocks of work were proposed for all civil and criminal work; a tightening of the merits test; and the establishment of the Community Legal Service were announced.

The Community Legal Service was intended to co-ordinate existing services such the Citizen's Advice Bureaux, Law Centres and other voluntary sector advice agencies. Lord Irvine said he wanted the Community Legal Service to facilitate 'the refocusing of the legal aid scheme as a tool to help poor people solve social welfare problems by gaining access to the justice system'. Under Lord Irvine, the numbers of not-for-profit agencies holding franchises increased substantially, growing from the initial 42 pilots started under Lord Mackay's tenure to over 400 by 2002/03.

Lord Irvine's speech to the Law Society also included announcements on the Lord Woolf proposals for the reform of civil justice, and an exemption from court fees for people on means-tested benefits. Lord Irvine announced a delay to April 1999 for the implementation of the Woolf reforms. The Woolf reforms were intended to reduce the 'cost, delay and complexity' of civil court proceedings.[5] When they were introduced, these new rules established the current Civil Procedure Rules (CPR), introducing protocols before starting court action, more active case management by the courts (including strict timetables for the preparation of cases), the wider use of alternative dispute resolution, as well as the division of cases into fast track for those under £15,000 in value and multi track for those above. The reforms also widened the areas of law in which conditional fee arrangements could be used. Generally it was concluded that the reforms worked well and now more cases are being settled prior to issuing court proceedings post-Woolf, [6] though this has had the effect of loading more costs onto pre-court work.

3   November 1997 *Legal Action* 3.
4   January 1998 *Legal Action* 3.
5   Lord Woolf, *Inquiry into Access to Justice,* Lord Chancellor's Department, chapter 3.
6   Department of Constitutional Affairs, *Further findings: a continuing evaluation of the civil justice reforms,* August 2002.

Backlash against the legal aid proposals

Lord Irvine's speech to the Law Society conference in 1997 set the tone for relations with the legal professions over the implementation of the government's legal aid reforms. LAG at the time said 'he was somewhat lucky to escape merely with a reduced ovation'. Throughout his time as Lord Chancellor, Lord Irvine was criticised for being arrogant and bullying[7] – this impression would not have been helped by him not engaging with the audience of solicitors at the Law Society, at least by taking questions after he made his speech. Steve Orchard was the Chief Executive of the Legal Aid Board at the time. He describes Lord Irvine as being 'really engaged with legal aid' in contrast to his successor. Orchard says he must have had over 50 meetings with him to discuss legal aid in his period in office. 'Irvine was the one who really got to grips with it', he says. Orchard concedes, though, that Irvine and the government could have done more to 'sell the policy'.

According to Orchard, the initiative to take civil compensation claims out of legal aid came from the government and not the Legal Aid Board. He says he had 'no issue with it as there had to be some prioritisation of what legal aid would pay for ... it was always by far the least worst option to save money'. Orchard, though, concedes that there were difficulties with the eventual scheme owing to the cost of insurance and the 'mark-up on fees'. Interestingly, Orchard also reveals that they had not looked seriously at competitive tendering in the Tory period, though it was discussed informally, as the Board had been mainly focused on introducing franchising as they were 'driven by the analysis they had no control over quality' and because of the lack of control over expenditure 'they had no room for huge policy changes'.

After Lord Irvine announced his proposals, they met with widespread opposition from outside government and the Legal Aid Board. A comment piece in the *Independent* in January 1998 was typical of the condemnation the proposals attracted:

> The legal aid budget will be restricted to cases in which compensation is not sought, such as criminal cases, injunctions or judicial review. The problem is this will not work ... Under a 'no win no fee' system, the loser in a court case still has to pay the winner's costs. Lord Irvine argues that lawyers should insure themselves against these costs but that will be a business decision about risk and complexity – not about justice.[8]

7   *Observer*, 5 April 1998.
8   *Independent*, 23 January 1998.

The following month Lord Irvine announced a watered-down version of his plans which were to be introduced in July 1998. 'No win no fee' would be introduced for all personal injury claims apart from medical negligence cases. Pressure groups had successfully argued that due to the high costs of investigating medical negligence claims it would have been impossible for potential claimants to find solicitors willing to take the cases on. In his announcement of the provisions, Lord Irvine said:

> We want to focus taxpayers' money where it is most needed and do the most good: on social welfare matters – employment, housing, debt, state benefits and actions against officialdom and bureaucracy.[9]

In defending the proposals before the House of Lords, Lord Irvine argued that the extension of conditional fee arrangements would result in £69 million being made available for social welfare law cases in 1999/2000, rising to £100 million by the following year. At the same time he also floated the idea of extending legal aid to employment tribunals. This proposal was predictably met with protests from employers and was eventually dropped.

Both the Bar Council and the Law Society objected to the proposals on personal injury cases. They were joined in a coalition of professional bodies, consumer groups and LAG opposing the changes. Law Society President, Phillip Sycamore, said:

> The abolition of legal aid in personal injury cases will hit poorer litigants hard. Conditional fee agreements may help some clients who will be denied legal aid, but they will not be able to help all. There will be many people with deserving cases who will be denied justice.

The proposals were also condemned by the Conservative Party opposition – Conservative MP Edward Garnier called them 'socially divisive, economically illiterate and politically inept'.[10]

Access to Justice Act 1999

Lord Irvine was central to piloting through the changes in the legal aid system brought in under the Access to Justice Act 1999 and the Immigration and Asylum Act 1999. The Access to Justice Act represented the biggest shake-up of legal aid legislation since 1948. It replaced the Legal Aid Board with the Legal Services Commission (LSC) and changed the rules on conditional fees. The Act also established the Criminal Defence Service (CDS) and included a provision

9   *Times*, 13 February 1998.
10   *Times*, 13 February 1998.

for salaried defenders. This was a controversial measure which had been taken out when the bill had been in the Lords as they were concerned that about the impartiality and independence of employed lawyers.[11]

Ministers – particularly David Lock, the Minister of State at the Lord Chancellor's Department – were enthusiastic about the establishment of the Public Defender Service (PDS) and ensured that the rules on salaried defence services were put back in a the final reading stage in the Commons. The PDS service proved more expensive to run than established private practice services. This was mainly because the offices, when they were established, had no client base. Both the LSC and practitioners acknowledge that the pattern in the establishment of new criminal firms is that the solicitors starting the firm either bring 'a following of established clients' or have to build this up while undertaking other work. According to Richard Collins, former head of policy at the LSC, without this the PDS was always going to struggle to be more economical than private practice: 'Particularly in the early days the PDS was much more expensive than private practice. Now we have shut down some offices it is more comparable in terms of cost.'

As well as helping understand the cost base of criminal legal aid, the PDS gave the LSC a 'plan B' if insufficient numbers of practitioners in an area opted to join the CDS by applying for a block contract. It would have been prohibitively expensive to establish PDSs in a large number of areas, but the establishment of a few acted as a warning to private practice that there was an alternative.

The most far-reaching change the Access to Justice Act 1999 introduced was a cap on overall expenditure. Until this point, as discussed above, the Legal Aid Board had controlled expenditure by altering scope and eligibility. The Legal Aid Board had mastered the art of predicting expenditure and lobbying the treasury to fund increases when they went over budget. The change to a capped budget and a determination by the Treasury not to allow expenditure to exceed this was to have great significance in later years, and as is discussed below, it is the main reason behind the retrenching in the second phase of New Labour and legal aid. For now, though, we turn to the other reforms introduced by Lord Irvine.

---

11   See June 1999 *Legal Action* 4.

Specialist quality marks and block contracts

Franchising – or the 'quality mark' system as it was to become – and contracting were an important continuity in policy between the previous Conservative regime under Lord McKay and New Labour. On taking office, Lord Irvine implemented plans that had been drafted under the Conservatives to make it compulsory to hold a specialist quality mark in order to apply for a contract to undertake legal aid work.

The Law Society opposed these changes, but was largely ineffective as it was engulfed with internal difficulties in this period, which had begun in 1995 with the election of Martin Mears as president on a platform of cutting back what he saw as an overly bureaucratic and unrepresentative organisation. His election split the Law Society's ruling council and the in-fighting culminated in accusations of bullying by Law Society staff against vice-president Kamlesh Bahl. Bahl eventually resigned in March 2000 and brought claims of racial and sexual discrimination against the Society.[12]

The Law Society had been officially neutral on whether firms should apply for franchises. With the Legal Aid Board's decision to make franchises compulsory for those firms wanting to provide green form/legal help work from January 2000, the Law Society was forced to come off the fence. The Law Society Council agreed in September 1998[13] that all firms should apply for franchises. It remained opposed, though, to contracting. In response to the publication of the Access to Justice Bill, the Law Society President Michael Mathews argued that legal aid should not be restricted to contracted firms as this would reduce client choice.[14]

A significant number of criminal law firms split with the Law Society to carry out negotiations over block contracting with the Legal Aid Board and participated in a pilot block contracting arrangement. A steering group of firms from Manchester and London had been formed late in 1997 to do so.[15] Steve Orchard admits that he always cultivated parallel relationships with the larger legal aid firms in order to get feedback on policy changes 'as due to the years of turmoil solicitors felt that they had no voice'.

12 Clare Dyer, 'Day of reckoning', *Guardian*, 27 November 2000.
13 *Law Society Gazette*, 30 September 1998.
14 *Law Society Gazette*, 25 November 1998.
15 Rachel Halliburton, 'Firms go it alone in LAB pilot talks', *Law Society Gazette*, 3 December 1997.

From 1 January 2000, firms and not-for-profit agencies had to have a quality mark in the relevant area of law to be awarded a civil legal advice and assistance contract. When the system came into force, around 5,500 contracts awarded were awarded to firms and organisations with franchises. Out of 52 Law Centres, 50 were awarded contracts. Citizens Advice Bureaux mainly received contracts in welfare benefits and debt. Robert Sayer, then President of the Law Society, condemned the changes:

> The legal aid changes are being introduced in a piecemeal and unco-ordinated manner. Overnight, the number of firms offering initial advice to clients on legal aid will fall from 10000 to 5000 with the contracting system, but the public will not know how to find the remaining sources of help. The Lord Chancellor's department is rushing into a grand experiment with the legal aid scheme – with the most vulnerable members of the public as its guinea pigs.

South London firm Mackintosh Duncan launched a judicial review against the system. The judicial review application was supported by the Law Society. Nicola Mackintosh, the firm's co-founder, said:

> We are willing to do the work for our clients. We need to be supported by the Legal Aid Board to do so, not prevented from providing our clients with the services they need. The board has a responsibility to ensure that vulnerable people have equal access to justice on the same footing as those able to pay for legal services. This scheme does exactly the opposite.

Mackintosh Duncan believed that the franchising scheme would have a detrimental impact on small specialist firms like themselves which specialised in mental health law, leading to clients being unable to receive the help they needed. The firm's arguments were that there was a common law right of access to the courts and that people had a right to chose who represented them. Despite having some sympathy with these arguments, the court found that there was no absolute right to have access to the courts or for the state to provide money to pay for a lawyer to represent. A further argument, that the scheme was irrational (mainly because, owing to the way it had been designed, it could potentially exclude specialist firms from legal aid) was also rejected on the grounds that the government was entitled to pursue the policy goal of reducing the cost of legal aid.

Soon after the implementation of the new contracts, Lord Irvine announced increases to civil legal aid funding, the first in four years. These were welcomed by the Law Society, the Housing Law Practitioners Association and the Immigration Law Practitioners Association among others, but criminal legal aid practitioners were annoyed that no increase for them had been forthcoming.[16]

Criminal Defence Service

Firms were asked by the LSC to decide whether they wanted to become part of the new CDS by applying for contracts which included police station work and representation in the magistrates' courts. These commenced on 2 April 2001. As with civil work, a quality mark in crime was compulsory for firms wanting to undertake the work.

Before the launch of the CDS, there were 3,500 firms offering criminal law advice and assistance. Just over 500 firms dropped out. Richard Miller, formerly Director of the Legal Aid Practitioners Group (LAPG), believes that most of these firms were only undertaking very small amounts of legal aid work and their dropping out of the system had little impact on services to clients. Miller also believes that the consensus at the time was that it was 'inevitable that quality marks would become compulsory'. Writing in *Legal Action*, South London Legal aid solicitor, June Venters, described the criminal block contracting pilot scheme as having worked well at her firm, but criticised how quickly the scheme had been introduced.[17]

In the run-up to the introduction of the CDS, Steve Orchard says that they were under much pressure to ensure that enough firms signed up to the scheme to ensure that it succeeded. There were protests by solicitors, including a threat of a 24-hour strike by some duty solicitors in November 2000[18] and a week of action in July 2000 organised by the LAPG.[19] Orchard was accused of using bullying tactics in the run-up to the introduction of the contracts, as he said in a letter to the *Law Society Gazette* saying that firms that did not sign the contract would not be able to undertake work after April 2001.[20] Large firms including Bindmans, Fisher Meredith, Hodge Jones and Allen, and Burton Copeland all said they were refusing to sign the contract.

Pay rises for civil work were announced in January 2001. They were largely welcomed by the firms and organisations, but they did cause some resentment from criminal practitioners. The following

16 'Mixed emotions as legal aid rates rise', *Law Society Gazette*, 24 January 2001.
17 August 1999 *Legal Action*.
18 'Striking solicitors fuel protest over criminal contracting', *Law Society Gazette*, 13 November 2000.
19 'Solicitors to strike for the first time over shake-up of Legal Aid system', *Independent*, 2 June 2000.
20 *Law Society Gazette*, 25 January 2001.

month, a pay rise – the first in eight years – was announced for crim-inal practitioners, and while some practitioners said that it would not be enough to persuade them to sign the contract, it seems it was enough to take the wind out of the protests. Orchard says it was given at the last minute as a tactic, to appear like a concession, so that the Law Society would give a clear recommendation to firms to sign the new contracts. According to Orchard, Lord Irvine and his adviser, Gary Hart, played a key role in orchestrating the strategy and tactics leading up to the implementation of the new contracts. Whatever the truth behind the tactics, it took further last-minute concessions, including the continuation of payments under the old structure for police station work, to persuade the Law Society finally to recom-mend that firms sign the contracts.

The introduction of compulsory specialist quality marks and con-tracts did dramatically reduce the numbers of legal aid suppliers, particularly in civil legal aid. Most commentators agree, however, that despite the reduction in access points, judged overall, the quality marks improved both advice and management standards. Both the private and not-for-profit sectors admit that the quality mark gener-ally benefited non legal aid services as well, as it impacted on the management of the whole organisation.

The main drawback to the new contracts was that for the first time suppliers were capped on the amount of work they could undertake. Private practice firms were allocated a maximum number of cases they could undertake, or 'matter starts' as they were called. Most con-tracted not-for-profit organisations (some Law Centres had private practice contracts) were provided with cash to pay for posts to under-take 1,100 hours of work per full-time caseworker, which the LSC considers reasonable for a caseworker or solicitor to produce.

Community Legal Service

The new CDS mainly consisted of a repackaging of existing suppliers into a rebranded service under the criminal specialist quality mark, as well as integrating the budget for Crown Court and higher courts cases into the overall budget. In contrast, the Community Legal Ser-vice was made up of a core of specialist quality marked firms and not-for-profit agencies which overlapped with a much wider group of non-specialist services which were quality marked at information and general advice levels. In attempting to integrate all civil, general and legal advice services into a seamless service, the government was

breaking new ground. Five quality mark levels were eventually established: Self-help Information, Assisted Information, General Help,
General Help With Casework and Specialist Help. Quality marks
were also established for websites, telephone services and mediation
services. A website, 'Justask', was also launched, which gave information and sign-posted members of the public to providers.

The success of the not-for-profit pilots, previously discussed,
meant that Lord Irvine was able to preside over a further expansion
of not-for-profit organisations providing civil legal aid, particularly
in giving specialist advice in social welfare law cases. One year on
from the establishment of the LSC, Richard Miller, Director of the
LAPG, judged this as one of the factors in making the LSC a success: 'A lot of money is being diverted to not-for profit organisations,
many of whom are providing excellent advice on areas not touched
by solicitors'.[21]

From taking government in 1997, the Legal Aid Board and the
government worked on putting the meat on the bare bones of a
policy statement in the Labour manifesto committing the government to establishing the Community Legal Service. Thirteen regional committees were established in the first year of the government
to co-ordinate local planning of civil law services. Consisting of six
members, four appointed from outside the LSC, they were asked
to draw-up plans for discrete geographical areas – these usually followed unitary local authority boundaries and became known as 'bid
zones'. Using information such as figures for means-tested benefits,
they drew up plans for the provision of civil law services in their areas
and prioritised the needs for new services. For example, the West
Midlands Legal Services Committee found a high level of need for all
areas of law in Birmingham, but low levels of need in the rural area
of South Staffordshire.[22]

In May 1999, the government published a consultation on the
Community Legal Service in which it floated the idea of Community
Legal Services Partnerships (CLSPs) being established in every bid
zone to develop better local networks and to plan legal services. The
following year, CLSPs began to be established across the country.
By 2002 there were over 200 up and running. By 2002, the LSC was
employing more than 100 staff at a cost of £4 million to administer
them. Adam Griffith, policy officer at the Advice Services Alliance,

---

21 Victoria MacCallum, 'A year wiser?' Law Society Gazette, 20 April 2001.
22 Assessment of need for legal service, Report to the Legal Services Board 1998/99,
    West Midlands Legal Services Committee.

was sceptical about their value. Writing in *Legal Action* in February 2003 he said:

> The idea of local planning of legal services is one which has had support from many quarters for a long time. The problem is that it has been introduced in the form of CLSPs, without any significant resources to enable them to identify unmet needs, within a capped legal aid budget, and specifically within the most vulnerable part of that budget.

Immigration advice was not part of the CLSP planning, as from 2000/01 it was administered centrally by the LSC. From the latter part of the 1990s, mainly because of international conflicts, the numbers of asylum-seekers in the UK began to increase. The government responded to this by introducing a policy of dispersing asylum-seekers across the country to ease the pressure on housing and other public services in London. The Legal Aid Board/LSC had to increase numbers of immigration law providers across the country at a time when it was forcing out suppliers by requiring them to hold the specialist quality mark. They were largely successful in doing this, as advice and assistance cases increased from 87,363 in 1997/98 to a peak of 155,865 in 2002/03.

In October 1999 the government extended scope to cover representation before the Immigration Appellate Authorities. This was restricted to cases that met a new merits test, and to specialist immigration providers. The Lord Chancellor's Department and Legal Aid Board had fought an internal battle within government to secure this extension on human rights grounds, arguing that not to allow representation to people facing torture or death in their countries of origin was a breach of article 6 of the European Convention on Human Rights (right to a fair trial including access to legal representation). LAG welcomed the move, but also called for widening to other tribunals – but to no avail. The extension of legal aid to representation in asylum cases represented the largest expansion of scope since police station work in the mid-1980s.

In what was to prove to be a final flourish for both Lord Irvine and Orchard, small increases in eligibility for civil legal aid were introduced in April and September 2002. The April change brought 1.7 per cent of the population into eligibility, and in September the gross income cap above which people were not entitled to legal aid was raised from £2,034 to £2,250. While these changes meant that more people could claim legal aid, apart from the notable exception of immigration work, there were no additional funds for civil legal advice from the outset of the Community Legal Service.

Labour's reforms assessed

The main criticism that can be levelled at New Labour around the reforms ushered in by the Access to Justice Act 1999 is that the abolition of legal aid for personal injury cases killed off a system which provided good access to justice. For the majority of personal injury cases, legal aid amounted to a loan underwritten by the state which was recoverable. It was replaced by a market-driven conditional fee system which seems to have inflated costs and led to controversy over claims management companies.

The old green form scheme did have the effect of opening-up access to justice in areas of civil law previously neglected by solicitors, but often the work undertaken under the scheme was shoddy. While resisted by Law Society, the introduction of compulsory contracting and quality marks for the legal help scheme (the successor to the green form scheme) were mostly positive innovations which raised the quality and efficiency of services. This is something which is now readily admitted by legal aid solicitors. There was also a problem with a small but significant number of fraudulent claims under the green form scheme. It is difficult to assess the extent of this, but there were some successful convictions which undoubtedly tarnished the reputation of legal aid in the eyes of the public.

In 1993/94, the numbers of firms under investigation by the Legal Aid Board for fraud rose from 362 to 957.[23] The then Legal Aid Board had put extra resources into detecting and tackling fraud. There were some high-profile cases which attracted attention through the 1990s and early 2000s. In one case in 1997, a judge described the firm of Grosberg and Co as a 'den of thieves' – the firm had volunteered to distribute surplus EU meat and butter, getting the unwitting recipients of the EU's largess to sign a green form; they would then manufacture a case to 'justify' the claim. More than £1 million was fraudulently claimed by the firm.[24]

Matt Howgate, a solicitor and management consultant, worked for the Legal Aid Board in this period. He believes that the problem of fraud was 'a significant factor' in the decision to introduce compulsory quality marks and contracting. He points out, though, that apart from a problem of fraud in immigration cases which the LSC had to tackle in the early years of the Labour government, the

23 See: www.independent.co.uk/news/uk/legal-aid-scams-could-cost-millions-hundreds-of-solicitors-firms-face-fraud-investigations-jason-bennetto-reports.
24 'Legal aid partner jailed for "wicked" green form fraud', *Lawyer*, 8 May 1997.

number of incidences of fraud reduced after 2000, but the trials of the cases working through the system were still taking place and this could have led to a perception of a continuing problem.

Many viewed the Community Legal Service as no more than a New Labour re-branding of legal aid – 'rearranging the deck chairs on the Titanic', as one sceptic described it soon after its launch.[25] With the benefit of hindsight, credit should be given to the New Labour government for trying to introduce a more rational system of planning and organisation to the civil legal aid system. As a public service, legal aid had evolved in a haphazard manner. A post code lottery operated (and continues to do so), in which clients only received a service if a solicitor had chosen to set up a practice specialising in the area of law in which they needed advice, close to where they lived. The major drawback to the Community Legal Service was that while the LSC had created a bureaucracy that was identifying need and raising quality standards, there was not the political will to find the cash to expand the service when need was identified.

CHAPTER 5

The politicians take control 2003–2010

Change in leadership

A change in the political leadership at the top marked the beginning of a new phase in the development of legal aid policy under New Labour. In June 2003, Lord Chancellor Derry Irvine was dismissed by Prime Minister Tony Blair, and replaced with Charles Falconer QC. Blair sacked his old mentor and boss and replaced him with his friend and former flatmate. Falconer and Blair shared a mission, which was to shake-up the Lord Chancellor's Department (LCD). As a precursor to the abolition of the role of Lord Chancellor, Lord Falconer also occupied the newly created post of Secretary of State for Constitutional Affairs. On the day he was appointed, 12 June 2003, the Department for Constitutional Affairs (DCA) was created with a remit to uphold justice, rights and democracy.

Lord Irvine's departure was followed soon after by the departure of Steve Orchard, who had announced his plans to retire prior to Lord Irvine's abrupt departure. Orchard recognised that the legal aid budget was growing out of control in criminal work, and to lesser extent in immigration. In his final interview as Chief Executive of the Legal Aid Board, published in *Legal Action*, he said that the biggest cost driver was criminal legal aid, and this was being driven by government policy.[1] As Chief Executive of the Legal Aid Board and latterly the Legal Services Commission (LSC), Orchard personified the cross-party consensus, in which the able bureaucrat held the whip hand on legal aid policy rather than the politicians. The genesis of the policies and the drive to implement them was Orchard's and the

1 June 2003 *Legal Action* 7.

Legal Aid Board's. The key reforms of the quality standards, contracting and the opening of legal aid contracting to non-lawyer agencies, were not party political in design and implementation. However, over the next few years there was a decisive shift away from this approach.

Increase in legal aid expenditure

In 2001/02 the government published its spending plans for legal aid.[2] Over the next three years the government allowed for some modest growth in the overall budget, as follows:

- 20001/02: £1.717 billion (actual)
- 20002/03: £1.748 billion
- 20003/04: £1.819 billion
- 20004/05: £1.929 billion

By 2004/05 there was an overspend of around £190 million. Big growth areas of expenditure were magistrates' courts cases, high-cost criminal cases and immigration cases. Richard Collins, the former head of policy at the LSC, describes the increase in immigration expenditure as being caused by a 'toxic mix of the growth in asylum-seekers and having to grow the supply base of immigration practitioners'.

The headline-grabbing figure of £2 billion in expenditure on legal aid was reached in large part by subsuming Crown Court and higher courts cases into the overall budget and the growth in their cost. Prior to 2001/02, legal aid for Crown and higher court cases had been administered by the courts. By 2005/06 expenditure had grown to £695.5 million, which was 32.7 per cent of the overall budget.[3] In 2000/01 the year before the budget was taken over by the LSC, the cost of Crown Court and Higher Courts cases was £422 million, which would have been 24.3 per cent of the overall budget.

Lord Falconer, speaking to LAG in 2009, blamed lawyers for the increase in expenditure, saying: 'Study any profession they will produce what will give them the most income. For example, if lawyers get money for the number of pages read, the number of pages read will go up.' His explanation for the increasing costs of criminal very high cost cases (VHCCs) in 1997/98 was that:

---

2   LSC Annual Report 2000/01.
3   *The justice gap: whatever happened to legal aid?* LAG, 2009 p147.

The Bar was using every part of the system to get as much as possible. Fees are still too high and cases are lasting too long. They are no more complicated than they were ten years ago.

Falconer uses the example of IRA terrorist cases to illustrate the argument that cases are no more complex than they were, and argues that for a jury to follow the evidence trial times need to be of reasonable length.[4]

The end of regional planning

Because of the increasing costs of legal aid, commentators were gloomy about the future. LAG in April 2003 predicted:

> ... despite all the changes and upheaval of the Access to Justice Act 1999 and the introduction of contracts, we may about to see the government return to using cuts in essential entitlements as a method of controlling the legal aid budget.[5]

Unfortunately LAG was right. An early casualty of the need to find cuts was the demise of the Community Legal Service Partnerships (CLSPs). Richard Collins admits that in 2002/03 the senior managers in the LSC took the decision to pull back from involvement in the CLSPs as they were 'very much Steve's [Orchard's] policy'. He says that at their height they were employing 130 staff to undertake the work. 'It made no sense at a time when there were falling numbers getting legal help to spend all our time joining up services ... Our view was that regional planning and partnership were not delivering.' Orchard argues that the CLSP policy had mainly been driven by the LCD and while he felt they did an 'excellent job ... the need for them dropped away'.

The final nail was driven into the coffin of local planning of legal aid services by the appointment of Sir Michael Bichard as Chair of the LSC in April 2005. Soon after joining, he took the decision to kill off the regional planning committees. Bichard says: 'They were not delivering very much. There was a moribund feel about the Commission, with members spending 40 per cent of their time in regional meetings which were of no benefit to providers or clients'.[6]

The loss of the regional presence at the LSC consolidated power in a central London bureaucracy. Without the counter-balance of

4 *The justice gap* p49.
5 April 2003 *Legal Action* 3.
6 *The justice gap*, p51.

influence from the regions and local providers, this made it easier for the LSC to disengage from suppliers' interests and concerns, to pursue a strategy of becoming a procurement agency rather than the administrator of the legal aid system.

The Fundamental Legal Aid Review (FLAR) was announced by the minister with responsibility for legal aid, David Lammy, in May 2004. At the same time, the government announced measures to cut £70 million from the criminal legal aid budget – including the introduction of a means test for legal aid in the magistrates' courts.

The FLAR was intended to be a wide ranging review which was to examine the root causes of the increases in expenditure in the system and to look at innovative ways of delivering the service in the future while giving value for money. Significantly, the Prime Minister's Strategy Unit provided assistance, and government departments including the Home Office and the Crown Prosecution Service, as well as others with an interest in the system including providers, were also consulted.[7] However, no final report was published. It seems that the report was buried as it did not reach conclusions that were politically acceptable. Lord Falconer says:

> The FLAR produced nothing. It did not come up with the fundamental change necessary. It did not address the issue of increasing costs of criminal legal aid ground into the system. Without this criminal would eventually end up taking the entire budget.

A fairer deal for legal aid, published in July 2005, included a reference to the FLAR saying that the paper sets out the conclusions of the review.[8] In reality, the paper provides the background and terms of reference for the Carter Review, discussed below. It is a classic piece of change management strategy – rather like the firm or organisation that has unpalatable options around restructuring which impact on employees, outside management consultants were brought in to deliver the unwelcome message. It is clear that the Carter Review was set up to provide a report to justify the introduction of competitive tendering.

Within the Commission, the use of competitive tendering for criminal services had been seen as the solution to controlling costs, or at least arriving at a market rate for the provision of services, for some time. A pilot for the London region was planned in 2005, but was fiercely opposed by suppliers. Sir Michael Bichard says: 'London competitive tendering was highly unpopular. To have any chance

7   DCA News Release, 'Legal aid review to target funds effectively', 17 May 2004.
8   DCA, *A fairer deal for legal aid*, CM 6591, TSO, July 2005, p17.

of convincing people we needed an objective independent review as it was clear the profession was not going to accept competitive tendering.' He recalls that one of his first discussions with Lord Falconer around the time he took over at the Commission in April 2005 was about who was available to undertake such a review. Lord Falconer says:

> It was my decision to get Lord Carter to undertake a review. I also appointed Michael Bichard as he could manage change. We had to break the hold of the criminal practitioners and force them to restructure so we could get more control over the costs of provision.

The Carter Review

In ordering the Carter Review, Lord Falconer was following in the long line of reports and reviews to find the solutions that have beset legal aid since its inception. Falconer's main policy concern was the 37 per cent increase in criminal legal aid since Labour came to power and the 24 per cent decrease in civil (not including asylum) and family legal aid.[9] He hoped that the Carter Review would set in train the introduction of 'best value tendering' (BVT) which would lead to savings to boost spending on civil work. He had no room for the expansion of the budget as the Treasury had set a ceiling of £2 billion on legal aid expenditure, which held until the cutbacks introduced by the current coalition government.

Lord Falconer believed that from the mid-1980s the Treasury saw legal aid as a big item of expenditure and that the 'LCD was trying to keep the system alive ... the state had discovered that legal aid was not subject to the same rigor of other areas of public expenditure'. Prior to him arriving at the LCD, he says that there was 'a real determination by the Treasury that the Department should keep to its DEL (Departmental Expenditure Limit)'.

Within the Commission there was disagreement over whether the Carter Review was necessary. Tony Edwards, a partner in the specialist criminal firm TV Edwards, oversaw the introduction of the Criminal Defence Service (CDS) as an LSC Commissioner. He believes that nearly every aspect of Carter was wrong. In what he saw as deliberate snub by the LSC,[10] despite being the Commissioner

---

9 See Lord Falconer's introduction to *A fairer deal for legal aid*, 2005.

10 Jon Robins, 'We wouldn't have had Carter if we'd been more worldly-wise', interview in *Independent Lawyer*, June 2007.

responsible for criminal legal aid, he was not consulted by Lord Carter while he was undertaking his research. The indications are that the senior staff at the Commission were already convinced of the need to introduce price competitive tendering. The limited study that had been carried out by Frontier Economics the previous year had concluded that competition was needed in the market 'to avoid the need to predict a set of efficient prices'.[11]

On the civil side of the LSC, policy was developed in parallel to the ongoing Carter Review. 'Making legal rights a reality' was published in July 2005. It outlined a draft strategy for civil legal aid and was largely welcomed by commentators. Controversially, though, it proposed the provision of joint tenders with local authorities for social welfare and family law services. To justify the policy, the Commission drew on the Causes of Action[12] research published by the Legal Services Research Centre. While the research does support the contention that clients face clusters of problems, it is based on a survey of the general population and not the group eligible for legal aid. Figures from the Ministry of Justice show that the numbers eligible for civil legal aid have continually declined under New Labour, down from 52 per cent of the population in 1998 to 29 per cent in 2007.[13]

Lord Carter published his report, *Legal aid: a market-based approach to reform*, in July 2006. Its main recommendations were:

- Criminal:
  - Redraw duty solicitor schemes into larger boundaries and introduce block contracts for police station work.
  - Introduce fixed fees for police station work.
  - Develop a graduated fee scheme for magistrates' court work.
  - Reform the fees paid in Crown Court cases.
  - Establish panels to bid for high cost cases on a BVT basis.
  - A spending cut of 20 per cent in Crown Court cases and a re-balancing of work away from the senior to junior Bar.
- Civil:
  - Fixed or graduated fees for all work.
  - Introduce a unified contract for all civil work, and limit contracts to either £25,000 or £50,000.

---

11 Nony Ardill, 'When in doubt, review it', June 2004 *Legal Action* 6.
12 Pascoe Pleasence et al, *Causes of action: civil law and social justice. The Final Report of the first LSRC survey of justifiable problems*, TSO, 2006.
13 Answer to parliamentary question by Dr Ahok Kumer, *Hansard* 20 February 2008.

– Introduce BVT for all civil contracts, with suppliers bidding against criteria including quality.

Lord Carter acknowledged in the report that some organisations would have to merge or discontinue legal aid work as the market consolidated. He argued that the transition to competitive tendering must be managed carefully.[14]

LAG has argued for some years that much of the evidence from the contracting for criminal legal aid services in North America indicates that there are reductions in quality and the creation of cartels which lead to an increase in costs. For example, in San Diego criminal defence service costs rose by 65 per cent after the introduction of competitive bidding.[15] The American Bar Association has also highlighted the increases in prices and concerns over quality, which has followed the introduction of competitive tendering.[16]

Much of government and LSC thinking on the costs of criminal legal aid assume that lawyers are to blame. Professors Ed Cape and Richard Moorhead undertook research on the cost drivers in criminal defence work. They concluded that 'decisions taken beyond the remit and direct influence of the LSC and of defence lawyers have had a significant effect on criminal legal expenditure, and account for a significant proportion of the increase in expenditure over the last decade'.[17]

Towards BVT – fixed fees and the unified contract

In preparation for the introduction of BVT, the LSC introduced a system of fixed fees for all civil and criminal legal aid work. A new contract was also introduced for suppliers which did away with the two different types of payment. Transitional arrangements were put in place for the not-for-profit suppliers which had originally been paid for blocks of work, using a funding formula based on the cost of producing the work, as opposed to hourly rates.

The LSC originally wanted to introduce the contracts and fixed fees in April 2007, but decided to postpone the introduction of the

---

14 Alison Hannah, 'Restructuring legal aid: the final Carter report', August 2006 *Legal Action* 6.

15 Roger Smith, *Legal aid contracting: lessons from North America*, LAG, 1998 p6.

16 Roger Smith, *Legal aid contracting: lessons from North America*, LAG, 1998 p30.

17 Ed Cape and Richard Moorhead, *Demand induced supply? Identifying cost drivers in criminal defence work: A report to the Legal Services Commission*, July 2005.

fees to later in the year after pressure from the Ministry of Justice. This meant that the reforms were undertaken in two stages.

The first stage of introducing the unified contracts went ahead. Solicitors threatened to boycott the introduction of the contracts. In March, a poll by the Law Society showed that 11 per cent of solicitors were not intending to sign the contract and 47 per cent were considering not signing it.[18] The Law Society also issued advice from its legal advisers not to sign the contract.[19]

Law Society Chief Executive Desmond Hudson said at the time: 'It is unfathomable that the government is still pushing ahead with these perilous reforms in their current form. It must stop being so cavalier about the risks to the legal aid system and reconsider the so-called reforms before it's too late.'[20]

The Constitutional Reform Committee reported on the Carter reforms the following month and described them as a 'breathtaking risk'.[21] The Law Society successfully won a reprieve on the introduction of fixed fees in criminal legal aid in judicial review proceedings. This threw the LSC into disarray. It eventually decided to give notice of termination on the existing criminal contracts and re-tender them to start from 13 January 2008. For some firms this was the last straw. Fisher Meredith, a large London-based firm, decided it no longer wished to undertake criminal legal aid work. Stephen Hewitt, a partner in the firm, estimated the fixed fees would mean a 9 per cent reduction in pay for police station work and a 16 per cent reduction in fees for magistrates' court work.

While the LSC deny this, it was concerned large numbers of solicitors would refuse to sign the new contracts. In the second showdown of the New Labour period, both sides played a game of brinkmanship over contracts, but again the firms cracked and signed in large numbers. The LSC later reported that 95 per cent of private practice firms had signed the contract. There was no attempt to organise a boycott from the not-for-profit sector, other than the Law Centres voting to threaten to boycott at their annual general meeting in 2006,[22] mainly as they were concerned about the impact of fixed fees. All the Law Centres signed the new contract.

---

18   Victoria Johnson and Catherine Baksi, 'Contract rebels pile pressure on LSC', *Law Society Gazette*, 29 March 2007.

19   Victoria Johnson, 'Unified decision', *Law Society Gazette*, 22 March 2007.

20   Victoria Johnson and Catherine Baksi, 'Contract rebels pile pressure on LSC', *Law Society Gazette*, 29 March 2007.

21   *Implementation of the Carter Review of legal aid*, 18 April 2007.

22   Law Centres Federation annual general meeting, 10 November 2006.

Civil fixed fees were implemented in October 2007 for civil legal aid. Richard Jenner, Director of the Advice Services Alliance, said at the time: 'Agencies that are geared towards doing many straightforward cases will be fine. Our concern is those agencies that undertake complex cases and/or cases for clients with language difficulties, disabilities or other special needs are going to struggle.'[23] Law Centres have faced such difficulties. For example, Stockport Law Centre closed in November 2007, citing the pressure from the change to fixed fees.[24]

BVT delayed

The reform programme hit significant problems. Despite 2,300 joining the specialist criminal panel, only 130 agreed to the new contracts on offer in March 2008. In what has been described as a 'grubby little deal' by Andrew Keogh, then a partner at Tuckers solicitors,[25] barristers who did not join the panel could still be instructed by solicitors, but the solicitors would have to negotiate the rates. They could retain the difference if the rate paid was lower than the fee paid by the LSC to the solicitors.

The Law Society won a judicial review in November 2007[26] on the legality of the civil legal aid contract. The decision in the judicial review led to an agreement between them, the Ministry of Justice and the LSC. The main points of the agreement were:

- no price competitive tendering until 2013;
- small rises in the rates paid in cases;
- no recouping of payments over six years old by the LSC;
- a closed list of Community Legal Advice centres and networks for the period ending April 2010;
- BVT for criminal delayed until July 2009.

It was around this time the LSC's view of BVT appears to have shifted. Carolyn Regan became Chief Executive of the LSC in 2007 after Clare Dodgson, Steve Orchard's immediate successor, who was forced to leave because of health problems. LAG reported in August 2008 that

23 October 2007 *Legal Action* 4.
24 January 2008 *Legal Action* 5.
25 April 2008 *Legal Action* 4.
26 *R (Law Society) v Legal Services Commission and Lord Chancellor and Secretary of State for Justice (interested party); Dexter Montague & Partners (a firm) v Legal Services Commission* [2007] EWCA Civ 1264.

Regan had said there were 'no savings predicted' from BVT. She was speaking at a press conference to launch the LSC's response to the consultation on the plans to introduce BVT for police and magistrates' court work.[27]

Straw takes over at the new Ministry of Justice

The DCA turned out to be short-lived incarnation of the old LCD, as the Ministry of Justice was established in April 2007. Lord Falconer had failed to abolish the ancient office of Lord Chancellor – it had proved too difficult to unpick the role of Lord Chancellor from the many statutes in which it is embedded. He continued as Lord Chancellor and then as Secretary of State for Justice, controlling a new department considerably larger than its predecessor.

The Ministry of Justice had taken over criminal justice functions from the Home Office, most significantly the National Offender Management Service (NOMS), which includes the prisons and probation services. Some had concerns over the creation of the Ministry of Justice – Lord Phillips of Worth Matravers, the then Lord Chief Justice, remarked: 'structures are required which will prevent the additional responsibilities taken over by the new Ministry [of Justice] interfering with or damaging the independent administration and proper funding of the court service'.[28] Despite this, the government pressed ahead and created the new department. The Home Secretary at the time, John Reid, seems to have been the main force behind the change. He wanted the Home Office to concentrate on security and combating terrorism by getting rid of the troubling distractions of prisons and probation.[29]

Lord Falconer's hold on the reigns of power at the new Ministry of Justice was tenuous, since as a close confidant of Tony Blair he was always unlikely to make the transition to a Gordon Brown led government, such was the enmity at the heart of New Labour between the Brown and Blair camps. After Blair's resignation as Prime Minister, and Brown's assent to the top job, Brown's first cabinet reshuffle saw Falconer replaced in June 2007 by the great political survivor of the New Labour era – Jack Straw.

27   August 2008 *Legal Action* 4.
28   Statement by the Lord Chief Justice, 29 March 2007, see: www.judiciary.gov. uk.
29   Michael Zander QC, 'Why was the creation of the Ministry of Justice railroaded through?' *New Law Journal*, 27 July 2007.

Straw had a brief career at the Bar before moving to the media and then into politics, becoming Labour MP for Blackburn in Lancashire in 1979. Like his successor Ken Clarke, he is a professional politician to the core, not a lawyer-turned-politician like Falconer. The addition of the prisons remit to the Ministry of Justice increased its political significance, as penal policy is an area never far from controversy. On taking over at the Ministry of Justice, Jack Straw seemed to have an outdated view of legal aid, believing that the system was being abused by fat cat lawyers, an opinion no doubt reinforced be the stories of fraud discussed in the previous chapter. According to one official, 'his views on legal aid were at least ten years out of date'. He had famously, while Home Secretary, attacked 'BMW-driving civil liberties lawyers',[30] and his fellow barrister and former boss Tony Blair had referred to the need to 'end the legal aid gravy train' in his conference speech in October 2003. This belief that legal aid lawyers were overpaid was part of the reason that the government continued to pursue BVT as a method of controlling expenditure and by extension lawyers' pay. This dominated the last two years of Labour's tenure of the legal aid system.

Independence and decision-making

Relations between officials at the top of the LSC and the Ministry of Justice were extremely poor in this period. Many officials around at the time describe a damaging personality clash between the LSC Chief Executive Carolyn Regan and senior officials in the Ministry of Justice. This was fed by differences over BVT policy and a desire from the politicians to exert more control over the LSC. No one is prepared to go on the record, but former officials at the LSC complain about pressure being exercised by the politicians over individual cases. This they say had happened under previous governments, but got worse in the later years of the Labour administration. A former official at the LSC said: 'Derry [Irvine, former Lord Chancellor] said that he wanted information including sight of the counsels' opinion on the gulf war veterans' cases. We said no, as this was improper, a position which he completely accepted. Jack Straw's regime crossed the line.'

One of the advantages of the LSC (and its predecessor the Legal Aid Board), being a separate agency with its own governance, is that individual decisions on entitlement to legal aid can be made inde-

---

30 Nick Cohen, 'Let's kill half the lawyers', *New Statesman*, 6 November 2000.

pendent of the government. LAG believes this is important to preserve the separation of powers between the executive and judiciary.
Many cases can involve government departments or have political
implications which might mean that the government has an interest
in not allowing access to the legal system which legal aid provides.
The separation of policy and decisions in individual cases which the
current system provides for, prevents interference in decisions by the
politicians and the perception of bias in decision-making on entitlement to legal aid in controversial cases.

Former LSC officials were particularly unhappy about what they
saw as political interference in high-profile and sometimes controversial cases. The Gurkhas' case caused much political embarrass-
ment for the government, with the actress Joanna Lumley backed
by the firm Howe & Co fighting a savvy media and legal campaign
on behalf of the British army veterans in their struggle to secure
settlement rights in the UK.[31] According to sources at the LSC, there
was much unhappiness among ministers over a press release which
highlighted the role of legal aid in the Gurkhas' successful case. This
contributed to the already strained relations between officials at the
top of the Ministry of Justice and the LSC.

In another example of the political heat that this case generated,
Howe & Co were the subject of parliamentary questions on what they
were claiming from the legal aid fund to represent the Gurkhas from
the then Conservative opposition.[32] A number of senior figures at the
LSC believed that the government overstepped the mark by attempting to interfere with the decision to grant the Gurkhas legal aid. A
former official at the LSC said: 'It was wholly wrong for David Keegan
[head of high cost cases at the LSC] to be summoned to a meeting at
the Ministry of Justice to explain why the case was funded. Ministers
changing rules is legitimate, but not looking at individual cases'.

Lord Bach was the minister responsible for legal aid from 2008 to
the general election in 2010. In an interview for this book, he denied
that there had been any improper influence on ministers over individual cases on his watch: 'I believe ministers and the department
[Ministry of Justice] should have responsibility ultimately for deciding what is in scope, but the politicians should stay out of decisions
in individual cases.' In the case of British peace campaigner Maya
Evans, it emerged that Lord Bach had been subject to some heavy

---

31   See, for example, the story by Patrick Wintour on Immigration Minister, Phil
     Woolas, being confronted by Joanna Lumley, *Guardian*, 7 May 2009.
32   Henry Bellingham *Hansard*.

pressure from the Ministry of Defence, and it is hardly credible that the purpose of this was not to influence the decision on the case rather than an overall policy.

Maya Evans brought challenges against the government over the treatment of detainees from Afghanistan. Her cases were brought in the public interest and she did not derive a direct personal benefit from them. She had successfully brought a claim concerning the handover of prisoners held by the UK to the Afghan intelligence services to 'a notorious torture centre in Kabul'.[33] The Defence Minister, Bob Ainsworth, in a letter sent to Lord Bach in November 2008, stated that he'd wanted the rules changed as he feared the consequences of an 'adverse judgement' in such cases. The Ministry of Justice went ahead with rule changes to the legal aid scheme to prevent further cases, and Evans challenged this in a judicial review. In a judgment highly critical of the government, the court found:

> For the State to inhibit litigation by the denial of legal aid because the court's judgment might be unwelcome or apparently damaging would constitute an attempt to influence the incidence of judicial decisions in the interests of government. It would therefore be frankly inimical to the rule of law.[34]

It was clear from emails from the Ministry of Justice quoted in the judgment that part of the reason that the department wanted to change the rules was to prevent potentially politically damaging judgments and that it was doing this at the behest of the Ministry of Defence. According to the email record quoted in the judgment, a meeting was held on 16 June 2009 between Lord Bach and officials 'to discuss access to legal aid for Iraqis and Afghans to support JR actions against the Government for actions by the British armed services ... Both Lord Bach and the Justice Secretary wished to see speedy progress made on this ...'.

This is so specific in its intent that it is difficult not to conclude that the line between policy decisions and decisions on individual cases was not crossed, or at least became very blurred, in cases involving Iraqis and Afghans detained by the British armed forces. The issue of independence in decision-making on cases was to become a significant one during the passage of the Legal Aid, Sentencing and Punishment of Offenders Bill through parliament. Lord Bach was

---

33   Daniel Carey, 'Torture legal aid case is a triumph of the rule of law', *Guardian*, 12 May 2011.

34   *R (Evans) v Lord Chancellor and Secretary of State for Justice* [2011] EWHC 1146 (Admin).

to redeem himself as a stout defender of the principle, but though an important concession was made on independence on decision-making, LAG is not convinced that there is sufficient protection in place. The tail end of the New Labour period in office illustrates the need for complete independence in decision-making in both appearance and reality.

A final fling

In Lord Bach's words, 'the LSC experience had not worked' and there was a need to establish clear responsibility for decision-making in legal aid policy. While in government he had also changed his view on social welfare law. As a former criminal defence barrister he readily admits to not seeing the importance of it until he had spent a few months in the position of minister responsible for legal aid. He was fearful legal aid costs in criminal cases would mean that social welfare law and the rest of civil legal aid would always be in competition with criminal legal aid for money, and because of the necessity of criminal legal aid being maintained to comply with the Human Rights Act 1998, this was a battle it was always likely to lose. He says Jack Straw and he believed that the solution was to establish two separate legal aid funds, something the Access to Justice Act 1999 allowed for, but which was never implemented, and that responsibility for policy-making in legal aid should be 'brought in house' to the Ministry of Justice.

In what was to be New Labour's final fling in legal aid policy, Straw called in the former senior civil servant Sir Ian Magee in October 2009, to undertake a review of the legal aid system and its governance (the 'Magee Review'). Behind the scenes, ministers had tried to persuade Magee to recommend a separation of the legal aid fund to protect civil legal aid, but he had not been convinced, though in his final report he did acknowledge that there could be an argument for doing so with social welfare law. In the report, which was published in March 2010, Magee did recommend that responsibility for policy should be the Ministry of Justice's alone, as ministers had wanted, but he acknowledged as his review went on, there was an increasing shift of emphasis to the financial management at the LSC.[35] In October 2009 the National Audit Office had found that just under

---

35 See Ministry of Justice, *Review of legal aid delivery and governance*, March 2010, p4.

£25 million in solicitors' fees had been claimed incorrectly. Magee found serious weaknesses in the LSC's forecasting and other financial management systems, with a myriad of different models and tools used to monitor expenditure. The government responded to his report by announcing its intention to reorganise the LSC, which required primary legislation. The LSC's Chief Executive, Carolyn Regan, resigned her post in response to the report and at short notice Carolyn Downs, a senior civil servant in the Ministry of Justice, was drafted in to replace her.

A continuing battle

Magee did acknowledge the government's success in controlling legal aid expenditure, and most importantly the cost-drivers in the system, something which LAG has consistently tried to highlight. New criminal offences and legislation such as the creation of Working Families' Tax Credit and the Mental Health Act 2007, were given as examples by Magee of having a knock-on impact to the legal aid budget. The government attempted to keep ahead of such increased costs by re-introducing means testing in criminal cases and introducing fee cuts. The attempt to bring in BVT for magistrates' courts and police station work was abandoned in July 2009. The government tried to press ahead with a pilot scheme in Somerset and Avon and Greater Manchester, but this too was shelved as the general election loomed.[36] Partly in response to this, Jack Straw decided to cut fees for Crown and higher courts work, as well as introduce a flat fee for police station work. In Lord Bach's words, 'we were seeking to reduce criminal fees in criminal legal aid in the minutes up to the Prime Minister going to the palace' to fire the starting gun for the general election campaign. Nine days before the general election, fees in Crown Court cases were cut by 4.5 per cent, to be followed by a further 13.5 per cent cut in the following two years.

In their final year in office, New Labour also attempted to introduce re-designed civil legal aid contracts. Bidders for social welfare law contracts had to satisfy the LSC that they could provide services in housing, benefits and debt, while family law contract bidders were given preference if they members of both the specialist chidcare and domestic abuse panels. The new criteria for family contracts had a devastating impact on the potential number of providers. If the

36 See *LAG legal aid handbook 2011/12* p320.

decisions on the tenders had not been challenged in a judicial review brought by the Law Society and others, the number of firms undertaking family work would have reduced from 2,400 to 1,300. The case, which was decided by Lord Justice Moses and Mr Justice Beatson,[37] hinged on the late notice the legal profession had been given over the selection criteria of panel membership.[38] The judgment was given in September 2010 and meant the new government had to accept they should allow the civil legal aid suppliers to continue much as they had done prior to the redesigned tender process.

37   CO/9207/2010, 30 September 2010.
38   See *LAG legal aid handbook 2011/12* p330.

CHAPTER 6

Coalition proposals for reform

Two old bruisers and a lightweight

The Secretary of State for Justice and Lord Chancellor

Soon after the ink was dry on the coalition agreement between the Conservatives and Liberal Democrats, announcements were made about the cabinet portfolios. Allocating the cabinet positions was a more complex task than usual, as they all had to be signed off by both parties to the coalition. There were a few surprises.

Six days after the general election, Kenneth Clarke arrived at the Ministry of Justice on 12 May 2010, and gave an impromptu speech to staff saying he only knew an hour ago himself that he was going to get the job of Secretary of State for Justice and Lord Chancellor. He had been Shadow Secretary of State for Business, Innovation and Skills and had expected to get this or another economic portfolio, but one of the problems Prime Minister David Cameron and Deputy Prime Minister Nick Clegg faced was finding a suitable slot for the able and popular Vince Cable, who was put in charge of the ministry Clarke had shadowed.

The appointment of Clarke made sense politically for a number of reasons. He is highly experienced, and Cameron probably felt that he would add gravitas to what remained a relatively inexperienced cabinet. He was also seen as a liberal-leaning Conservative, and most significantly he is pro-Europe. This latter attribute proved most damaging to his prospects of ever becoming leader of the Tory party, but made him an obvious choice for Liberal Democrats wanting to ensure balance to a cabinet which could be portrayed as Eurosceptic, or at best Euro-indifferent, among its conservative members. In the context of justice policy, his liberal instincts on penal policy also made him a natural coalition choice.

Douglas Hurd, a cabinet member under the Thatcher and Major governments, once remarked Clarke was 'the kind of politician who will cross a road in order to get into a fight'.[1] Who knows what his chances might have been in becoming leader if he had been more circumspect over his difference with many in his party over Europe. His combative style, though, had meant that he had forged a successful career under Margaret Thatcher's premiership, in cabinet portfolios which included introducing cuts in the big spending public services of health and education. The Ministry of Justice's budget is miniscule compared to that of the NHS – £9 billion as opposed to the £106 billion which is spent on health. Perhaps he viewed reducing the justice budget as a relatively easy task compared with the cuts he had been forced to find in the past. Deficit reduction is one of the defining themes of the coalition government, and arriving at his new department Clarke quickly set about looking at making cuts. He wanted to accomplish this task speedily, as once the budget was agreed, this would open his way to joining the cabinet committee which oversees the spending plans of other departments.

According to Matthew Elliott, Director of the Taxpayers' Alliance, a memoir by the former Chief Secretary to the Treasury, David Laws, reveals the Justice Secretary had little grasp about the detail of the £350 million in cuts which he was agreeing to, saying to Laws, 'What are you asking for again? Three-something isn't it? Yes, absolutely, I'll look at it but I'm sure it won't be a problem'.[2] Perhaps Clarke's casual remark is not surprising as he famously does not do detail. Unfortunately, the minister with responsibility for legal aid does not do so either.

The minister

Jonathan Djanogly was elected to the constituency of Huntingdon in 2001, replacing the former Prime Minister, John Major. He is the son of a millionaire industrialist and worked as a partner in a City law firm before becoming a Member of Parliament. In opposition he held various positions including Shadow Solicitor General and Shadow Business Minister in the team shadowing the Department

---

1   Matthew Tempest, *Guardian*, 10 August 2001.
2   Matthew Elliott, 'Spending cuts at Ministry of Justice', *Daily Mail*, 30 January 2012.

for Business, Innovation and Skills under Kenneth Clarke. After the general election in 2010 he followed his old boss to the Ministry of Justice and was made Parliamentary Under-Secretary of State at the Ministry of Justice responsible for legal aid and civil courts reform. He left the government in September 2012, after a cabinet reshuffle.

According to a number of sources in the Ministry of Justice at the time, Djanogly's political views were to the right of his boss: 'he is very pro free market and is in favour of rolling back the state' they said. As a politician, Djanogly has proved to be somewhat accident-prone. He demonstrated poor political judgement in using private detectives to investigate whether key Conservative members in his constituency party were hostile towards him in the wake of controversy over his expenses claims. Even his own parliamentary agent, Sir Peter Brown, was one of the senior Tories investigated by the private detectives he hired. According to the *Telegraph*, the report prepared by the detectives quoted one senior source in the Conservative Constituency Association as saying: 'He has been a disaster and we need to deselect him, but it will take time'.[3]

Still, the episode did throw up one of the funnier asides in the fight against the Legal Aid, Sentencing and Punishment of Offenders (LASPO) Bill. Over a dinner at the Law Society, Djanogly complained that someone was posting spoof tweets on Twitter which were attributed to him. Peter Lodder, the then Chair of the Bar, suggested that in order to deal with the mystery, he ought to hire a private detective to investigate. Lodder insists his comment was made entirely innocently and was surprised by the sniggers it caused around the dinner table as well as the slightly miffed look from the minister.

Djanogly's woes, caused by in large part by his own misjudgment, led to continual gossip that he was not up to the job and would go at the next reshuffle.[4] Some of this is of course the standard cut and thrust of politics in which getting the man or woman instead of the ball is a fairly standard tactic. During the passage of the LASPO Bill through parliament, Djanogly was criticised for failing to declare his children held shares in his brother-in-law's claims management companies. This resulted in him being stripped of the responsibility for overseeing the regulation of these companies.[5] This, and the other

3 'Jonathan Djanogly "should consider his position" over use of private detectives', *Telegraph*, 10 September 2010.
4 Neil Rose, 'Jonathan Djanogly: moribund in a dead end job', *Guardian*, 21 October 2011.
5 *Telegraph*, 4 October 2011.

controversies which have followed him, have meant that he has had to toe the line and was unlikely to be able to persuade Clarke to go for the politically riskier option of introducing competitive tendering for criminal legal aid, discussed below. The consequence of this was that by far the highest portion of the cuts would fall on civil legal aid.

As a man, Djanogly is polite and personable. He was said to be 'liked by his officials' as he sticks to his prepared notes.[6] In other words, he does not stray off-message.

It would be something of an understatement to say legal aid is not an area of policy which engages him. Throughout the passage of the LASPO Bill he did the minimum to defend the government's policies, largely just reading out the briefings his civil servants had prepared for him. For long periods of time when the bill was in committee, he left it up to government backbenchers of the committee scrutinising the bill, to defend it. He was more at home speaking in favour of part two of the bill, which dealt with the reform of litigation funding and costs. His lack of interest reached its nadir with the debate on Labour's amendment to do with the industrial disease, mesothelioma – a disease caused by exposure to asbestos – and Djanogly was caught on camera grinning and giggling while an amendment was proposed to bring such cases back into the scope of legal aid. The Shadow Justice Secretary, Sadiq Khan, said: 'His smirking and giggling showed utter disrespect to sufferers of this horrific disease'. Djanogly explained his mirth by saying he had been laughing at another minister who had forgotten his notes.[7] Perhaps Labour's anger at the incident was slightly overblown, but it does support the image of Djanogly as something of a liability to his own party.

The peer

Much of the work on developing legal aid policy was carried out by Kathryn Laing, Kenneth Clarke's special adviser. In the early days of government, Laing asked officials: 'Why don't we just privatise legal aid?' It had to be pointed out to her that legal aid had always been, and remains so, practically a 100 per cent privatised service as the bulk of it is carried out by firms of solicitors and self-employed barristers.

6 Neil Rose, 'Jonathan Djanogly: moribund in a dead end job', *Guardian*, 21 October 2011.

7 Jason Beattie, 'Tory minister "smirked and giggled" during asbestos victims debate', *Daily Mirror*, 19 April 2012.

According to civil servants, Clarke came into office with ideas about legal aid 'caught in the mid-nineties as if the previous Labour government had never happened', viewing the legal aid budget as bloated and as something which could be cut with little damage to the fabric of the justice system. His most radical idea, which was welcomed by his Liberal Democrat coalition partners and penal reformers, was to cut the numbers of prisoners, the so-called 'rehabilitation revolution' to which the coalition agreement committed the government.[8] He was supported in this policy by Lord McNally, the Liberal Democrat peer, who, like Clarke, can be described as something of a political bruiser, in contrast to the more lightweight Djanogly.

Lord McNally was a career labour politician born in Blackpool, Lancashire. After working in senior jobs with the Labour Party, he was elected MP for Stockport South in 1979, before defecting to the Social Democrat Party (SDP) in 1981. After boundary changes, he contested the new seat of Stockport at the 1983 general election as the SDP candidate and was defeated. He was raised to a peerage in 1995, and became Minister of State at the Ministry of Justice in 2010 after the coalition government was formed. It is clear McNally played little or no part in the formulation of legal aid policy, but when the LASPO Bill reached the House of Lords, in his dual role of Justice Minister and leader of the Liberal Democrats in the Lords he was to have a central role in getting the bill through, including the use of some strong-arm tactics, discussed below. Lord McNally is described as getting on well with Kenneth Clarke by both officials and political sources and was 'very annoyed' by Number 10's intervention on penal policy in the early stages of the formulation of the bill. Like many of his Liberal Democrat colleagues, Lord McNally seemed to have made the calculation that Clarke needed his support 'to keep him in position whatever his faults as the right of the Tory party had wanted Michael Howard as Lord Chancellor'.[9]

Michael Howard's views on penal policy are at odds with reformers, including Clarke, as he believes that 'prison works', a claim he made while he was Home Secretary in 1992. While not clashing directly with Clarke, he claimed on the BBC Radio 4 Today programme in response to Clarke's plans when they were published in December 2010: 'We have seen a very significant increase in the prison population since 1993 and an almost halving of the crime

---

8 Coalition agreement, May 2010 p23.
9 Anonymous Liberal Democrat speaking to the author.

rate. These two things have gone together – they are connected'.[10] The disagreements within the Tory party over penal policy led to the interventions from Number 10 which so annoyed Lord McNally. One result of this was the 'early release' scheme which Clarke had proposed for offenders who pleaded guilty being vetoed, at a cost of around £140 million in budget savings, putting more pressure on the need to find cuts in legal aid, which is the second largest item of expenditure in the Ministry of Justice's budget.[11]

An old idea

The coalition agreement included a commitment to 'carry out a fundamental review of legal aid to make it work more efficiently'. It was an unfortunate choice of words, as there had already been a Fundamental Legal Aid Review (FLAR) under Labour's Lord Falconer in 2004, but this FLAR had not led to any final report, but had instead given way to the Carter Review (see previous chapter). In contrast to previous reviews, the coalition's review was not an open process. It took the form of civil servants looking over previous legal aid policy initiatives and trying to gather fresh ideas on the direction of the system, including alternative methods of funding it.

While in opposition, the then Shadow Justice Minister, Henry Bellingham MP, had in October 2009 outlined his plans for legal aid to LAG, if the Conservatives were to win the general election the following year. He told LAG he saw legal aid as 'one of the pillars of the welfare state' and that as the economy improves, the Conservatives if elected would like to bring in extra money to legal aid. They would also do this by looking at innovative ways to supplement the legal aid budget. His plans included borrowing an idea from France: 'La Carpa' is the French system of having one bank account held by the government, into which all the money French lawyers hold for clients is paid. The money in the account earns interest which goes towards the French equivalent of legal aid. Henry Bellingham said that as much as €300 million has been raised by the fund in the past, but admitted that because of historically low interest rates the amounts earned currently are much lower.

10   Alan Travis and Helene Mulholland, 'Prison system failing to tackle reoffending, says Clarke', *Guardian*, 7 December 2010.
11   'Mounting concerns over legal aid cuts', *BBC News*, 29 June 2011.

Promises made by politicians in opposition often prove to be worthless, and so it proved with Bellingham, who became a minister in the Foreign and Commonwealth Office after the general election, a safe haven from any accusations of hypocrisy over legal aid policy. While the civil servants did evaluate the French system and others, these ideas did not make the final bill.

A system to collect interest on client accounts to pay for public legal services – often referred to as an Interest On Lawyers Trust Accounts (IOLTA) scheme – is used in other common law jurisdictions, for example in Victoria, Australia, to fund public legal services. This seemed the most likely alternative source of cash for legal aid, but the government dismissed the idea in its response to the consultation on its proposals for legal aid (see chapter 7). The main reasons for not adopting an IOLTA scheme given by the government was the fluctuation in income and the existing practice of some firms donating the cash for charitable causes, including pro bono services. In the US, money generated by the IOLTA scheme has reduced from $370 million in 2007 to $92 million in 2009.[12] The Law Society argued that donations of interest should remain voluntary and the government said it had 'given considerable weight' to these views.[13] While not stated officially, it is likely that the government was put off pursuing the IOLTA option because of the complex legislation needed to introduce such a system, which would meet strong opposition from the Law Society and others representing lawyers' interests. With the dismissal of the IOLTA scheme, politicians became focused on making large cuts in legal aid from an early stage in the policy-making process.

Early controversy

Within weeks of getting his feet under the desk at the Ministry of Justice, Jonathan Djanogly faced a crisis as the large immigration law charity, Refugee and Migrant Justice (RMJ), faced collapse because of cash-flow problems. RMJ employed 350 staff and undertook over 10,000 asylum and immigration cases a year. The organisation had experienced cash-flow problems since the changeover to fixed fees for the not-for-profit sector in April 2009. They appealed to

12 *Reform of legal aid in England and Wales. Government response*, June 2011, p245.
13 *Reform of legal aid in England and Wales. Government response*, June 2011, p246.

the government to bail them out by reverting to paying for work in progress on cases rather than waiting until the case was closed. At the time, Caroline Slocock, RMJ's Chief Executive, told LAG:

> RMJ is not asking for new money, simply prompt payment of legal aid for the work it has carried out. Until recently we were given regular, ongoing payments for the work we do. As a [not-for-profit] organisation, we cannot expect to make sufficient profit to finance millions of pounds of working capital.[14]

Slocock had been working behind the scenes for months to try and persuade the government to rescue the organisation. Such a move was not without precedent, as the previous legal aid minister Lord Bach had been persuaded to put together a bail-out plan for South West London Law Centre in February 2010. A grant of £235,000 had been given by the Ministry of Justice to help the Law Centre survive by restructuring. To his credit, Lord Bach pushed this through despite opposition from civil servants who took the view the Law Centre was inefficient and should be allowed to fold.

According to Slocock, she had met Lord Bach and discussed RMJ's problems with him. Lord Bach said he would 'do something', but a few days after meeting him the general election was called. The resourceful Slocock, who had good contacts with the conservatives, having worked as a civil servant in Number 10 with Margaret Thatcher, tried to secure a meeting with Jonathan Djanogly, Lord Bach's successor, but to no avail. The minister was not for meeting.

With nothing to lose, RMJ went public with its campaign to persuade the government to save the organisation. Much effort went to into lobbying politicians and others and a high-profile media campaign was launched. A consortium supported by the Deputy Leader of the Liberal Democrats, Simon Hughes MP, was established to raise cash. It succeeded in raising £76,000 in 24 hours, but there was never any question that the minister, Jonathan Djanogly, would lean on his officials to find a way to help the organisation. His views were, 'Why are we funding them?' and that they are 'badly run'. RMJ was allowed to sink, leaving 10,000 cases to be reallocated among other providers, who were reluctant to take them on.

A year later, the Immigration Advisory Service (IAS) also went into administration. The organisation had experienced cash-flow problems similar to RMJ. It worked out of 12 offices across the country, and this time over 25,000 live cases were left to be reallocated.

---

14 'Refugee charity faces closure', July 2010 *Legal Action* 5.

Alison Harvey, General Secretary at the Immigration Law Practitioners Association, commented to LAG:

> Clients, including in areas where there is little or no alternative provision, struggle to find alternative representation. We know from members that the Legal Service Commission's 'bulk transfers' of Refugee and Migrant Justice files has left many lawyers with boxes of unclaimed files – they have never seen the client, and no alternative representative has ever called for the file. These people are unrepresented, and at risk.[15]

One senior official told LAG that ministers were not as susceptible to pressure from RMJ and IAS as the previous government might have been because they took the view that the coalition was going to get a bad press anyway for the first two years, and so they 'were not going to be bothered by bad stories in the press about charities closing'. The RMJ episode can be seem as the first illustration of an austerity machismo that developed amongst ministers and government politicians as the legislation on legal aid made its way through the parliamentary process. It would also seem though that the proposals on legal aid which emerged in November 2010 after the FLAR process were informed by some preconceived ideas ministers held about legal aid and the people it assists.

Civil legal aid targeted

Caroline Slocock believes, in retrospect, Jonathan Djanogly did not want to meet her to discuss RMJ's plight because he was aware at an early stage that his government was going to cut advice on immigration law. She says: 'This would have killed off RMJ anyway, whatever happened about our cash-flow problems because a high proportion of the work we undertook was on non-asylum immigration cases.'

Another indication of what was to come was the Legal Service Commission's (LSC's) decision in July 2010 not to go ahead with plans to sponsor training contracts for young legal aid lawyers. The decision on this had been delayed for over a year, but Laura Janes, the then chairperson of Young Legal Aid Lawyers (YLAL), told LAG:

> This was promised by the last government. The minister [Lord Bach] showed me the paperwork and said it was going to go ahead. It will be a bitter disappointment to many law students and newly qualified lawyers, as this was their last hope of a career in legal aid work.

15 August 2011 *Legal Action* 4.

Over the years, the LSC had sponsored the training of 750 lawyers in legal aid firms and some Law Centres. The scheme gave them a chance of getting a foot on the career ladder, and more importantly ensured that the legal aid system recruited talented lawyers at the start of their careers, rather than letting them go off to pursue more lucrative careers in commercial law. Ministers would have been consulted over the decision on the training contract grants, but it was clear they were planning to make cuts and so would not want to commit to training future legal aid lawyers.

A number of sources have told LAG that at an early stage of the policy formation process, the politicians received advice from a set of barristers' chambers with close links to the Conservative Party. The paper outlined what could be cut from the scope of the legal aid system without risking challenges under the Human Rights Act 1998, and set the parameters for what eventually emerged in the consultation papers published in November 2010. Looking at the options around cutting large parts of the civil legal aid scheme was not a new idea though, as civil servants had wheeled out similar suggestions under budget doomsday scenarios for the previous government. As discussed in the next chapter, private law family had been identified by the previous government as a potential area to cut, and social welfare law had been considered as an option. However, the advice the government received from the chambers seems to have contributed to ministers' early decision to go for large cuts in civil legal aid.

Kenneth Clarke and his ministers all seemed to share the view that the legal aid budget was bloated by over-generous payments to fat-cat lawyers. Of course this view was reinforced by the media stereotype of legal aid lawyers, which Labour had played a part in perpetuating, but it had nothing to do with the facts, as under the previous government the legal aid budget had been tightly controlled, and pay for lawyers in the system was at best static or in most cases reducing. Other preconceptions informed ministers' opinions. For example, a senior civil servant described Kenneth Clarke's understanding of domestic violence as 'being stuck 30 years ago'. His view of much of social welfare law was that it was not something lawyers should be paid to do. For example, when cutting housing disrepair cases from legal aid was discussed with him he is believed to have said: 'Why don't people just move if they don't like the home they are renting?' In private, Djanogly expressed more extreme views than Clarke, taking the line that people's civil legal problems were not something with which the state should be involved in assisting them.

Djanogly's free-market views led to the most significant clash behind the scenes over the formation of the policy which would form the basis of the consultation paper discussed in the next chapter. He believed that significant savings could be made from the legal aid budget by introducing competition for criminal work immediately. In part, this can be seen as a continuation of Labour's policy of best value tendering (BVT) for criminal legal aid which had been abandoned at the eleventh hour, but it also reflected his own political views and accorded with the thinking of many of the larger criminal firms who believe that they can make economies of scale by being able to tender for large volumes of work across police stations, magistrates' courts and Crown Courts. In the lead-up to the publication of the government's proposals for legal aid, sources close to the minister say that he pushed hard to introduce competitive tendering, but met resistance from the LSC who had concerns about designing a tendering system in a short timescale. Also, there were fears that savings from a competitive tendering process could not be guaranteed. Eventually his boss came down on the side of caution saying that competitive tendering should be delayed. It seems likely Clarke might have been swayed, in part at least, by the impact such a move would have had on his old colleagues at the criminal bar, as tenders would have most likely favoured large criminal solicitor firms, while the self-employed bar would have had to subcontract with these firms for work.

Losing his tussle over introducing competitive tendering for criminal work meant that the die was cast as regards the policy direction of the eventual LASPO Bill, as most of the savings would have to come from the scope of the civil legal aid scheme, though as discussed in the next chapter, cuts in fees to all legal aid practitioners made a contribution. Officials at both the LSC and the Ministry of Justice worked on options for making the necessary savings. What they came up with was much the same as had been discussed under the previous government. Lord McNally seems to have had little or no involvement, and the final decisions on what would be cut from scope were made by Clarke and Djanogly over the first few months of the coalition government. However, as discussed in chapter 8, McNally was to bear the brunt of the criticism from his Liberal Democrat colleagues.

CHAPTER 7

A rump service

The rumour mill

New Labour government

The legal aid minister under the previous government, Lord Bach, was to play a pivotal role in the opposition to the coalition government's plans for legal aid in his position as a shadow minister in the House of Lords. Lord Bach is a skilled political operator who knows the best way to win over his fellow peers is by reasoned debate rather than partisan political posturing. While being the minister responsible for legal aid is never a route to winning a popularity contest with his fellow lawyers, he was able to build bridges with the Law Society and the other groups representing legal aid providers through a combination of charm and a genuine commitment to access to justice. If Labour had returned to government, though, it was likely that they would have also made large cuts to legal aid, and Lord Bach had dropped hints about their likely plans while in office.

In July 2009 Lord Bach had called a meeting of all the main representative groups and others concerned with legal aid policy, including LAG. The purpose of the meeting, which was held on an off-the-record basis, was to discuss ways of saving cash in the legal aid system. The meeting heard a presentation from Carolyn Regan, the then Chief Executive of the Legal Services Commission (LSC) and Sarah Albon, who was responsible for legal aid policy at the Ministry of Justice. Their message was blunt: the legal aid budget was under pressure because of the impact of the recession, the Baby Peter case (which had led to an increase in child protection cases)[1] and the high volume of Crown Court cases; they said that they wanted to develop a co-operative approach to tackling this budget crisis.

At the time, Lord Bach told LAG that he believed they should have gone further at the meeting and discussed the stark policy options they were faced with. In Lord Bach's view, such was the pressure on the legal aid budget that it was likely that the government would have to look at big cut-backs in scope to satisfy the Treasury. Chief among the cuts which were being discussed in the department, he said, was the loss of all family law cases, apart from those involving care proceedings and child abduction. As previously outlined, the need to fund divorce cases was a major factor which had led to the establishment of the civil legal aid system after the Second World War, and it remained a large chunk of the civil legal aid system. Lord Bach's clear opinion was that expenditure on such cases could not continue, but the meeting back in July 2009 did not discuss this. Instead, it concentrated on suggestions around reducing experts' fees and efficiency savings in the courts system. While these options would save some cash, Lord Bach believed that they would have been unlikely to meet the target that would be set by the Treasury after the general election.

It is clear, then, that whichever political party or combination of parties had formed a government after the 2010 general election, it is likely that there would have been large cuts to the scope of legal aid, particularly in family work.

Coalition government

There was little communication between the new coalition government and the legal aid providers leading up to the publication of the consultation paper in November 2010. One provider organisation complained to LAG that despite publishing research relevant to legal aid in this period, they could not get a meeting with ministers. Owing to the controversy surrounding family civil contracts relations with the Law Society, the LSC and the Ministry of Justice were also at a low ebb. There was much speculation, though, about the likely scale of cuts. In September 2010, *Legal Action* published an editorial on the possible areas of cuts.[2] The article was based on briefings from

---

1   Shona Macleod, Ruth Hart, Jennifer Jeffes and Anne Wilkin, 'The impact of the Baby Peter case on applications for care orders', Research report, National Foundation for Educational Research, June 2010.
2   'The rumour mill', September 2010 *Legal Action* 3.

sources close to the Ministry of Justice and warned the cuts could be as much as £500 million and would target mainly civil legal aid.

LAG did meet with officials and the Minister Jonathan Djanogly in this period, but mainly to discuss the possible alternative methods of funding for the legal aid system. We shared a mutual problem, as both LAG and the Ministry of Justice had reached the conclusion that client account interest (see chapter 6) was probably one of the only realistic options to find additional money, but it was impossible to obtain an accurate estimate of what could be raised as the firms were less than forthcoming, not surprisingly, in giving details of their earnings from this.

LAG held two seminars with the conservative-leaning think-tank Policy Exchange, in July and September 2010. At these seminars, practitioners and experts on legal aid policy got together to discuss the possible options on a confidential basis. At the first seminar, a joint briefing paper from LAG and Policy Exchange outlined the stark options around legal aid cuts. Kenneth Clarke had indicated that about 25 per cent in cuts from the LSC budget would need to found and as this amount could not be found from the prisons budget a greater amount would need to come from the courts and the legal aid budgets. LAG took the decision to end its relationship with Policy Exchange after the second seminar, as the think-tank had a clear agenda of looking for cuts options with little thought to the consequences of these.

In October 2010 the government announced its Comprehensive Spending Review (CSR), which gave some hard figures to the rumour mill of likely cuts. For the Ministry of Justice the target for the four years of the CSR commencing in April 2011 was a cut of 23 per cent of its total budget, reducing its spending from £9.3 billion to £7.3 billion by April 2015. The planned cuts announced included a consultation on closing 157 under-utilised courts, a 33 per cent cut in administrative costs and a 50 per cent reduction on capital spending on prisons.

Proposals announced – worst-case scenario realised

When the announcement of the government's plans for legal aid was eventually announced, it represented the worse-case scenario for civil legal aid that LAG and other groups concerned with access to justice policy had feared.

Civil legal aid targeted

Proposals for the reform of legal aid in England and Wales[3] was published on 15 November 2010. The government was seeking responses to the paper by 14 February 2011 prior to introducing legislation in the spring of 2011. Out of a total of £350 million in cuts to legal aid outlined in the paper, £279 million would fall on civil legal aid (see appendix 7).

The main proposals outlined in the paper were:

1) Divorce and private law children cases to be cut from scope, saving £178 million.
2) Cuts in scope to non-family civil legal aid, including immigration, housing, welfare benefits, debt and employment, totalling £64 million.
3) A 10 per cent cut in all civil legal aid fees and in experts' fees.
4) A telephone advice line to be introduced to access the remaining civil legal aid services.
5) Changes in the structure of criminal fees and the introduction of price competitive tendering by 2011/12.
6) Confirmation of the government's intention to abolish the LSC and administer legal aid directly.

The paper also announced the government's intention to move to competition in the pricing of criminal services, but as discussed in the last chapter, Djanogly lost the argument over this behind the scenes and further delay was announced later in the year. Andrew Keogh, a solicitor and well-known commentator on criminal legal aid, speaking to LAG in December 2011 said: 'The delay to competitive tendering represents a ceasefire, but one that comes with risk. Large firms desperately need volume in order to return a decent profit and all firms desperately need other parts of the criminal justice system to reform and not pass on inefficiencies.' Keogh also believed that the delay gave the bar breathing space, as they would have struggled to tender for the work and would have had to have relied on solicitors instructing them to act in cases, and not to retain too much of the fee for advocacy. He argued that the government would continue the downward pressure on fees, leading to increased competition between the independent bar and solicitors for the shrinking advocacy market: 'The enemy is probably no longer the government, but each other. It will be a bloody ending for publicly funded criminal work.'

3 Ministry of Justice, Consultation Paper CP12/10, November 2010.

Together with the report, a comprehensive set of impact assessments were published by the coalition government. These outlined how the proposals would affect the users of the legal aid system. The assessments were used throughout the campaign against the government's proposals to defend legal aid, as they outlined starkly the potentially devastating impact of the government's plans for the system on the poor and people protected by equalities legislation (see chapter 8). Speaking in an adjournment debate in the House of Commons, called in response to the paper on 14 December 2010, Labour MP Karen Buck pointed out that people with disabilities would be 'disproportionately affected. For example, 63 per cent of legally aided clients in the sphere of welfare benefits assistance are disabled.' Concern over the proposals was not just confined to the opposition. Speaking in the same debate, Dr Julian Lewis, the Conservative MP for New Forest East, told MPs that he feared his local Citizens Advice Bureau would be forced to lose two part-time posts if the cutbacks were to go ahead. The impact of the cuts on the Citizens Advice Bureaux service and not-for-profit sector was of deep concern to many backbench MPs from all political parties.

According to the government's impact assessment, in total just under 550,000 people would no longer receive advice and representation in civil legal aid cases. The proposed cuts in the scope of civil legal aid also included an 83 per cent reduction in the number of family cases, a 36 per cent reduction in housing cases and a cut of 100 per cent for welfare benefits, clinical negligence and employment.[4]

A well-worn path

The government's main justifications for its proposals were outlined in the consultation document and did not change throughout the passage of the legislation through the parliamentary process. Jonathan Djanogly had given a flavour of these prior to the publication of the document the previous month at a fringe meeting at the Conservative Party Conference in Birmingham, organised by Policy Exchange. He had told the meeting that the government did not want to go down the road of another 'salami slicing review', that fees needed to be examined and, in a justification for the cuts which was to be heard many times, that England and Wales spent £38 per head of population on legal aid, much more than other countries such as the £3 spent in France and £5 in Germany.

4 *Legal Aid reform: scope changes*, Ministry of Justice Impact Assessment No 028, p16.

In citing higher costs of the legal aid in England and Wales, Djanogly was treading a well-worn path, as previous ministers had used these comparisons. Lord Bach, for example, in announcing the Magee Review had said:

> The UK has one of the most generous legal aid schemes in the world and the government is committed to ensuring legal aid is prioritised effectively so that more people are able to access it to resolve their legal problems. In the current climate, it is even more important that this public money is managed efficiently and effectively.

The press release including this quote then goes on to give figures for spending in other countries such as £8 per head of population in the Republic of Ireland compared to the £38 in England and Wales.[5]

Labour had commissioned a report from Roger Bowles and Amanda Perry of the University of York,[6] anticipating that the academics would confirm the UK's greater spend on legal aid compared to other jurisdictions. This research found that part of the explanation for the higher levels of legal aid spending was the higher levels of crimes and the greater number of criminal prosecutions brought to court in England and Wales. For example, they found that in Sweden the figure is 759 prosecutions per 100,000 population compared to 2,806 in England and Wales.[7] Most importantly, while the report did find higher levels of expenditure on criminal legal aid in England and Wales, this needed to be viewed in the context of overall spending in the courts system. For example, while France only spent €4.8 per head of population on legal aid, compared with €57.67 in England and Wales, once the other costs of the courts system were factored in the total cost was €51.40 in France compared with €80.48 in England and Wales. The Netherlands had a larger overall courts expenditure at €90.61 compared with England and Wales (see appendix 3 for the full table). Bowles and Perry concluded that the relatively higher cost of criminal legal aid in England and Wales compared with other EU countries 'appeared to be offset by lower court budgets and public prosecution costs'.[8] While they found that civil legal aid expenditure in England and Wales was greater than EU and other common law jurisdictions, at least part of the explanation for this was due to the higher number of divorces,[9] and as personal injury cases had been

5   MoJ press release, 'Review into the delievery of legal aid', 14 October 2009.
6   R Bowles and A Perry, *International comparison of publicly funded legal services and justice systems*, MoJ, October 2009.
7   Bowles and Perry (above) p24.
8   Bowles and Perry p27.
9   Bowles and Perry p31.

removed from the scope of legal aid (see previous chapter) this had led to a large reduction in gross spending on non-family cases in England and Wales.

International comparisons in public expenditure can be made across a large range of public services. Britain spends less per head of population on health services than its European neighbours, but we do not hear politician arguing that we need to increase expenditure to the levels of France's $3,978 and Germany's $4,218 per capita as opposed to the UK's $3,487.[10] They would probably be more likely to attribute the differences to factors such as a more efficiently run service. The use of international comparisons, as the academic Richard Moorhead has observed, was something which arrived in the rhetoric of the legal aid debate after Labour had managed to control the growth of the legal aid budget (as previously discussed) as a reason to justify further cuts.[11]

Campaigns launched

More than 5,000 submissions were lodged in response to the consultation – the vast majority of which were overwhelmingly hostile to the government's proposals – and two major campaigns were initiated to oppose the government's plans for legal aid. The first was by the Law Society. Insiders at the Law Society admit that they were initially slow to start lobbying against the proposals in parliament because of the loss of their Head of Public Affairs, Nicky Edwards, who had left the Law Society suddenly in July 2010. The Law Society also suffered from having poor links with Conservative politicians, and owing to the disarray caused by the loss of Edwards, had little contact with politicians before the committee stage of the bill. They used outside public affairs professionals to get their 'Sound Off For Justice' campaign off the ground, a campaign targeted at gaining support from the general public. This was combined with a lobbying effort after the bill was published, to oppose the government's plans. Around the same time, in January 2011, the 'Justice for All' campaign was launched by Unite the Union, charities including LAG, and other organisations and individuals opposed to the legal aid cuts.

10 OECD Frequently requested data.
11 See: www.publications.parliament.uk/pa/cm201011/cmselect/cmjust/681/ 681vw17.htm.

The Justice Select Committee, in response to the government's proposals, decided to hold an inquiry into them. Sir Alan Beith, Chairperson of the Committee and a Liberal Democrat MP, spoke at the launch of the Justice for All campaign on 12 January 2011, saying: 'We have to ensure there is support available for people going to tribunals'. He also said that 'while the government is not going to sign a blank cheque for legal aid in the future, support must be given to people most in need', and he called for organisations to put in submissions to the inquiry on the impact of the proposed changes to legal aid.

Both Justice for All and Sound Off For Justice felt that it was important to put clients at the forefront of their campaigns. At the launch of Justice for All, the meeting heard from a former legal aid client, Deborah. In an emotional speech she told the packed launch event, which was held in the House of Commons, that she and her daughter had been victims of domestic violence. They had been living in a women's refuge for a year, but after receiving advice from the housing charity Shelter they were re-housed. They used Shelter's legal service again when they experienced harassment from their neighbours. Deborah told the meeting that 'without Shelter and legal aid both my daughter and I would not be where we are today, in a good home'. Sound Off For Justice was instrumental in organising a large contingent of Gurkhas, who had used legal aid to challenge successfully the immigration rules (see chapter 5) to attend the large Trades Union Congress (TUC) rally against the government's public sector cuts at the end of March 2011. They were joined by Justice for All and other supporters on the march protesting against the legal aid cuts.

At the launch of Justice for All, impromptu speeches were made by the Shadow Justice Secretary Sadiq Khan MP and Shadow Justice Minister Andrew Slaughter MP. Sadiq Khan said that 'a justice system which is accessible to all is one of the pillars of a civilised society'. He told the meeting that if Labour had been re-elected to government it would have been forced to make cuts to legal aid, but echoing what was a key theme of the Justice for All campaign he said it would not have made them to social welfare law, as early advice in such cases 'saves money in the long term'.

Justice for All co-ordinated a day of action on 3 June 2011 to highlight the impact of the government's proposals for legal aid and other advice services cuts. Demonstrations and other events were held across the country. These included a rally in Sheffield addressed by the former Home Secretary, Labour MP David Blunkett, and marches in Birmingham and Coventry. Justice for All campaigners were successful in attracting support from members of the public and government MPs including the Conservative MP Amber Rudd. She told a rally in her Hastings constituency, attended by local Citizens Advice Bureau staff and other advice agencies, that she was willing to fight her own party if necessary, 'It's all about caring for vulnerable people. Both parties have agreed that there need to be cuts to the legal aid benefit system by £350 million over four years. But this is the wrong area that is being targeted.'[12]

In London a public meeting held outside the Supreme Court heard from speakers who included Marylyn Haines-Evans from the Women's Institute, 'The WI is well aware from our recent campaign on violence against women that legal aid is a vital, life-saving resource for women leaving violent relationships. Put simply without access to legal aid on a wide range of issues, women are more likely to stay in situations that are unsafe for themselves and their children.' This event and others received coverage in the national and local media raising the profile of the Justice for All campaign.[13]

Select Committee Report

Speaking at the All Party Parliamentary Group on Legal Aid on 30 March 2011 – the day the Select Committee Report was published – Robert Buckland MP said that 'the evidence base for the reforms is too narrow for what is proposed'. He also stressed that the total cost of the legal system, including legal aid and the courts system, was about the same as continental Europe, though he acknowledged that costs were greater than other common law countries. Buckland, who is the Conservative MP for Swindon South, was reflecting the views of the Justice Committee of which he is a member. He was critical of the government's proposals, but like the committee's report, stopped short of calling on the government to reverse the proposed cuts.

The committee accepted the need to reduce spending on legal aid, but put forward recommendations on how it believed the 'government's proposals should be refined'.[14] In LAG's view the report was

12 'Legal aid cuts hurt those who can't afford it', *Hastings and St Leonards Observer*, 14 June 2011.

13 www.justice-for-all.org.uk/dyn/1310484128414/jfa-dayofactionwriteup.pdf.

14 Justice Committee *Government's proposed reform of legal aid* Third report of session 2010–11, HC 681-1, 30 March 2011, p9.

very much the work of 'critical friends', rather than people prepared to upset the applecart.[15]

Sara Albon, Director for Civil and Legal Aid Policy at the Ministry of Justice, had given evidence to the committee. She said that expenditure on legal aid was mainly 'dictated by the volume of cases'. Albon in her evidence also acknowledged the difficulty in making international comparisons about cost and quality as it is 'difficult to find some other area, look at it and think they are providing a much better and cheaper service than us. Mostly, when they are spending a lot less, it is because they are buying a lot less'.[16]

The report gave a good summary of the cost drivers at work in increasing the numbers of cases.[17] Since 2006 there had been a rise of 26 per cent in Crown Court cases. Factors such as digital technology, which has increased the average page count of evidence in criminal trials by 65 per cent, has fed into increased costs. It noted that the Ministry of Justice had controlled the costs of criminal cases by measures such as reintroducing the means test for magistrates' courts in 2006/07 and in Crown Courts in 2010, but the committee argued that 'greater efficiency' in the courts could be achieved by agencies working together more effectively in the criminal justice system.[18]

In civil legal aid there has been a shift away from representation to legal help, though the report acknowledges the increase in public law family cases driven by the Baby Peter case. While the number of civil representation cases has fallen, expenditure on them has increased by 8 per cent in four years. The report found that:

> By contrast the 19% increase in spending on legal help over the last 10 years can be attributed to increased demand in areas of social welfare law, including debt, housing, employment, and welfare benefits. The Ministry of Justice and Legal Services Commission have found no evidence that the complexity of law has operated as an inflationary pressure for the costs of civil and family legally-aided work.[19]

As the majority of civil legal aid work is funded on[20] a fixed-fee basis, the report argued that the increasing costs were mainly driven by the rising numbers of cases. Factors such as the recession, LAG believes,

15   'Justice Committee legal aid report falls short', May 2011 *Legal Action* 9.
16   Justice Committee *Government's proposed reform of legal aid* (see fn 14) p18.
17   Ibid p12.
18   Ibid p25.
19   Ibid p12.
20   Ibid p24.

is at heart of this, and the report also acknowledged that there is little which can done to control these costs other than limiting the scope of legal aid.

A crucial finding of the committee was on the potential impact of the proposed legal aid cuts on other arms of the state. While it edged close to calling for the government to reconsider the proposed cuts in the scope of civil legal aid, it did not make this explicit. The report argued that for issues which have such an effect on peoples' fundamental well-being, simply cutting legal aid might well increase costs in other parts of the legal system,[21] and cited evidence from Citizens Advice about the cost of the legal aid cuts to the public purse.[22] It acknowledged that poor decision-making in government departments is a major cost-driver in legal aid expenditure. It pointed to the large increase in the number of social security appeals in 2008/09 as evidence of this, and stated that appeals were likely to rise to 370,000 that year (2010/11) and to 436,000 the next year (2011/12).[23]

In his evidence before the committee, Jonathan Djanogly said that the Department for Work and Pensions (DWP) already transfers some cash to the Ministry of Justice to cover the costs of the tribunal system caused by benefits changes. He revealed that a sum of £21.1 million – roughly equivalent to the cost of legal aid for welfare benefits – would be transferred to the Ministry of Justice in 2011/12 to help defray the costs to the tribunal service of the introduction of Employment Support Allowance. Djanogly did not, however, support the imposition of a charge on the DWP to support the costs of legal aid, arguing that this would be like 'robbing Peter to pay Paul' – but the committee were unconvinced by this argument. They found that introducing a charging policy would provide a 'financial incentive to public authorities to get their decisions right first time'.[24]

The committee called for evidence from Nick Hurd MP, the Minister for Civil Society, as it was particularly concerned about the impact of the cuts on not-for-profit services in social welfare law. Hurd gave evidence about the applications to the Transition Fund from advice organisations. The fund was set up to assist voluntary organisations hit by the public spending cuts and is now closed. The committee called on the government to offer another round of transition

---

21 Justice Committee *Government's proposed reform of legal aid* p19.
22 Ibid p54.
23 Ibid p26.
24 Ibid p27.

funding and to extend the grants for face-to-face debt advice beyond the year extension which was recently agreed.[25]

The LASPO Bill

Backbenchers from all political parties were concerned about the impact of the legal aid cuts on Citizens Advice Bureaux services and the not-for-profit sector, and this was to prompt action from the Prime Minister's office, which is discussed below. A source of great disquiet amongst many Conservative backbenchers was the Justice Secretary's perceived softness on penal policy. He had come into office with the promise of a 'rehabilitation revolution' and was intent on cutting prison numbers by introducing reforms which included a 50 per cent reduction in a sentence for a crime if the defended pleaded guilty early. After pressure from the right of his party, Prime Minister David Cameron decided to junk these changes just before a bill incorporating them, the legal aid changes and the reforms to the costs of civil litigation was due to be published. After a delay of two weeks from the original time-table, the altered bill was published on 21 June 2011. Its title was the Legal Aid, Sentencing and Punishment of Offenders (LASPO) Bill – the word 'punishment' having being added as a sop to the backbench critics of the Justice Secretary.

When the story of the Number 10 inspired U-turn on sentencing policy emerged, LAG and other commentators estimated that the Ministry of Justice would have to find up an extra £100 million in cuts to pay for the extra prison places. When Kenneth Clarke left office in September 2012, the numbers of prisoners had increased by 1,600 from when he had arrived at the Ministry of Justice in May 2010[26] and there is no clear indication how his replacement, Chris Grayling, is going to budget for the increase. According to the Liberal Democrat MP Tom Brake, in an interview for this book, 'any room for manoeuvre' in the planned cuts to civil legal aid were 'hit for six with the loss of remission allowed for guilty pleas'. Other Liberal Democrat sources described the Liberal Democrat Minster of State for Justice Lord McNally as being furious over the capitulation by the Prime Minister to Conservative right-wing opinion on penal policy.

---

25   Ibid p50.
26   Frances Gibb, 'Reshuffle means Grayling ushers in a new era as a non-lawyer in justice post', *Times*, 6 September 2012.

The substance of the final bill as regards legal aid was much the same as had been consulted on. The bulk of the cuts would fall on civil legal aid. However, some ideas had been dropped, including the suggestion of charging all clients with £1,000 of disposable capital £100 towards the cost of their legal aid; and the proposal to use client account interest to subsidise legal aid. The government had also realised that it was vulnerable over the impact of the planned cuts in social welfare law and the effect this would have on not-for-profit advice centres. Justice for All, charities and, above all, the only people who really matter to a government trying to get a controversial bill through parliament – backbench MPs – had made their voices heard on this issue. During the debate on the second reading of the bill – which is the point at which MPs formally debate a bill for the first time – Kenneth Clarke announced a fund of 'up to £20 million' to pay for Citizens Advice Bureaux and other not-for-profit agencies providing advice in housing, debt, employment and benefits.

While it was Kenneth Clarke who announced the Advice Service Fund, the policy process over the formation of the fund took place in the Cabinet Office. In February LAG and the Baring Foundation had organised a conference of not-for-profit providers with the Cabinet Office. The event was well attended by the sector and government departments. Speakers and other participants had been unequivocal in their message to the government that the sector was facing an unprecedented crisis because of the combination of the threatened legal aid cuts and the pressure on other funding such as from local authorities. The Cabinet Office sits at the centre of government and attempts to manage policy across Whitehall on behalf of the Prime Minister and cabinet. A number of sources have told LAG that there had been concern expressed about the impact of the changes to legal aid by members of the cabinet and Clarke's announcement was clearly a culmination of a co-ordinated effort to assist the sector. LAG received a call on the day of the second reading of the bill from Kathryn Laing (Clarke's special adviser) to brief about the announcement. She assured us that the cash was 'new money' to offset the impact of the cuts on advice services from legal aid and other funding sources. Laing and others close to the government deserve credit for the part they played behind the scenes in securing the money. This was motivated by a mixture of real concern, especially for the impact of the cuts on Citizens Advice Bureaux, and the cold political calculation that the Bill would face problems if nothing was offered to the Citizens Advice Bureaux service and not-for-profit sector in general to offset the cuts. If the fund for advice services is disregarded, it has to be said that the legal services lobby made no significant impact on the government's proposals. The bulk of the cuts, £178 million, fell on family legal aid and as this was an option which had already been under active consideration by the previous government, the new administration must have felt they could hold the line on this.

Previous governments, such as in 1986 (see chapter 2), when wanting to cut the legal aid bill had used changes in scope and eligibility, but by introducing the LASPO Bill the coalition government were less likely to get embroiled in legal challenges to its plans, such as that which had derailed the family law tenders. Above all, owing to a combination of the priority to implement austerity measures and key ministers' dismissal or, at least indifference to the need for much of civil legal aid, the government was attempting a radical reshaping of the legal aid system. The bill's intention was to move it decisively away from what legal aid had evolved into since the early 1970s – from a safety-net legal service working like a fifth pillar of the welfare state, to a rump scheme to cover people accused of a crime and civil cases for the poorest in which human rights were directly engaged, with the bulk of the civil system covering child protection cases. With the publication of the bill, the scene was set for a debate in parliament over this much reduced vision of the future of state aid for access to justice.

CHAPTER 8

Campaigners get their ducks in a line

The LASPO Bill in the Commons

Campaigners got an early opportunity to challenge the minister on the detail of the Legal Aid, Sentencing and Punishment of Offenders (LASPO) Bill, as the week after it was published the minister responsible for legal aid policy, Jonathan Djanogly, attended the All Party Parliamentary Group on legal aid (legal aid APPG). Law Society President Linda Lee summed up the feelings of the audience, which mostly consisted of lawyers and not-for-profit organisations, when she said: 'I am disappointed and heartbroken; this attack on civil legal aid is an attack on the most vulnerable.'

She went on to question why the minister had not taken up any of the Law Society's suggestions regarding alternative sources of funding for the legal aid system. In total these options exceeded the total cuts at £394 million[1] – admittedly some (such as the cap on barristers' fees) might be more headline-grabbing attempts than a serious policy choice, but suggestions such as the levy on the financial service industry to pay for the cost of fraud cases which would raise an estimated £92 million, deserved serious consideration. The minister responded by saying: 'Much of what was suggested by the Law Society was to get others to pay for legal aid. When you go to the Treasury, it is not so keen on creating new taxes'.

The legal aid APPG had been established by the Legal Aid Practitioners Group (LAPG) and the Young Legal Aid Lawyers (YLAL). All Party Parliamentary Groups are a useful vehicle to engage MPs and peers on specialist issues. The legal aid APPG was able to increase

---

1 Catherine Baksi, 'Law Society sets out £394m justice system saving', *Law Society Gazette*, 17 February 2011.

its work during the passage of the bill mainly because it received a small grant from the Baring Foundation, an independent charitable trust. The Baring Foundation also agreed a substantial grant to LAG to employ a full-time campaign worker for the Justice for All campaign. Gail Emerson and Will Horwitz were employed in the role of Campaign Manager from August 2011. They played a considerable role in increasing the profile of the campaign and helped focus the efforts directed towards influencing parliamentarians.

Like the Law Society, Justice for All was slow to get off the ground, particularly in the early stages of the bill. With hindsight, more should have been done by organisations concerned with legal services to try to counter the negative perception of legal aid among many parliamentarians sooner. Speaking to LAG after LASPOA 2012 was passed, Desmond Hudson, Chief Executive of the Law Society, spoke about the difficulties in persuading MPs that legal aid 'was not about money-grabbing lawyers'. With the Baring Foundation grant for the Justice for All campaign and the considerable resources the Law Society (they are rumoured to have spent around £300,000 on their Sound Off For Justice campaign alone) the campaign against the bill managed to get its ducks in a line over the summer of 2011, ready for the party conference season and the return of parliament.

Going through the motions

There are a good few lawyers stalking the corridors of power at Westminster and it was hoped that some would draw on their experience as practitioners to argue against the detail of the LASPO Bill. An example of an MP who did this was Helen Grant, the Conservative MP for Maidstone and The Weald. She was a legal aid lawyer specialising in family cases before entering parliament at the 2010 election. During debates on the bill she made a number of helpful interventions, for example in the second reading of the bill she was critical of the proposal for a telephone gateway:

> The plans have telephone advice as an alternative to a trusted and recommended solicitor, but the law is complicated. The law can be an ass, and it is not easy to understand. Having tried to explain maintenance pending suit or some other aspect of the Matrimonial Causes Act 1973 to a frightened and vulnerable litigant, I can tell Hon. Members that it makes clients feel frustrated and confused and leaves solicitors feeling quite inadequate.[2]

2   See: www.publications.parliament.uk/pa/cm201011/cmhansrd/cm110629/debtext/110629-0002.htm.

Throughout the course of the bill's progress through parliament, Grant was especially concerned that the plans for legal aid would 'badly impact on women'[3] and raised these concerns behind the scenes. In February 2011 she wrote an article for the *Guardian* in which she nailed her colours to the mast regarding her views on the LASPO Bill:

> Over the last three decades the distance between the haves and have-nots has increased, and our society has weakened due to the demise of the family unit and the rise of the benefits culture. These are ailments that will take some time to cure; but to stem the flow of legal aid while we are in such a critical condition, amid a stifling recession, could prove devastating.
>
> Experience shows that members of the public are not well-equipped to represent themselves on a legal stage. Technical issues of law and procedure aside, it is virtually impossible to maintain composure and focus when you yourself are the subject of litigation. Further, self-representation will most likely fall to those least capable of planning or articulating their case. And let us be clear about who these cuts will affect: a third of legal-aid clients who have received advice on debt, and a staggering two-thirds of those needing advice on benefits, have an illness or disability. It cannot be right that those most in need of support are left without it.[4]

However, Grant stopped short of voting against the government, possibly with an eye to the promotion she later secured (she was made a minister in the Ministry of Justice after the reshuffle in September 2012). Her interventions in the early stages of the bill probably marked her out as someone the government whips could not rely on in the committee stage of the bill.

The committee stage of a bill in both the Commons and the Lords is the point in the process at which a bill receives detailed scrutiny from parliamentarians. Amendments are proposed to the bill in this stage in the Commons and can be voted on, though they are frequently withdrawn by the opposition so that they are permitted to be tabled at a later stage of the bill. The government has an inbuilt majority on the committee and often this is used to force through bills with little real debate. Unfortunately, for opponents of the LASPO Bill the government whips had done their job and packed the committee with MPs who were not going to stray from the government line.

---

3 See Hansard (fn 2 above).
4 Helen Grant, 'Legal aid is the last line of defence', *Guardian*, 2 February 2011, available at: www.guardian.co.uk/commentisfree/2011/feb/02/legal-aid-last-line-defence.

After LASPOA 2012 had been passed, LAG spoke with an experienced parliamentarian. What had struck many campaigners against the bill was that many Conservative and Liberal Democrat parliamentarians, though having expressed misgivings about the bill both in private and public, had trooped through the lobbies in support of it. When this was put to this particular politician, their response was: 'No matter how decrepit or incompetent they might be, never underestimate a politician's capacity to delude themselves that if they tow the line they might secure advancement'. The power of patronage is an important weapon to enforce party discipline and it is especially potent with the type of more junior politicians which made up the government's supporters on the LASPO Bill Committee.

The Labour opposition on the committee was led by Andy Slaughter MP, Shadow Justice Minister and a barrister. Like many members of the Bar, Slaughter can tend toward the verbose in his speeches; however he deployed this to good effect in the first days of the committee stage in order to give more time to prepare amendments over the summer recess. Sometimes in Westminster politicians can act as if they have complete distain for their opponents, but it would be fair to say with regards Slaughter and his opposite number Djanogly, this was not an act and debate in the committee was sometimes bad tempered. Much of the time the process felt like a political charade, with both sides going through the motions – Djanogly particularly made little or no effort to engage in debate, and true to form merely read out briefings prepared by his civil servants, leaving his colleagues such as Ben Wallace MP to do the work of taking on the opposition.

The committee stage though did act as an opportunity to rehearse the main lines of argument against the bill and build support for amending specific sections of it. When the committee returned from the summer recess, Labour members of the bill committee moved a number of amendments which were intended to reverse cuts the government had proposed – these included an amendment from Andy Slaughter to reinstate legal aid in medical negligence cases and one from Kate Green MP, who proposed an amendment which would widen the definition of domestic violence. This was a move supported by women's rights groups including Rights of Women and the Women's Institute. Plaid Cymru's member of the committee, Elfyn Llwyd MP, also gave notice of a number of amendments. Most of the amendments proposed did not proceed to the vote.

While no votes were lost by the government in the committee stage of the bill, it seemed that there was an expectation on the government's side that they would be facing difficulties getting the bill through the Commons without substantial amendment. Ben Gummer MP, a Conservative member of the committee told LAG when asked about amendments to the bill on the definition of domestic violence and the need for an independent appeals system on decisions on granting legal aid, that he agreed they were issues that needed addressing. However, Gummer told LAG they were not something the committee would deal with, saying 'these are matters for the House of Commons', implying that a vote on them would be taken by the whole House. Talking to other government supporters at the time, it was clear that even if the Commons did not vote to amend it, they believed that the House of Lords would deal with the difficult detail of the bill and amend it if necessary, before sending it back to the Commons. It seemed that the government strategy was to hold the line on the bill and not to offer any significant concessions until they were forced to do so by peers.

Liberal Democrat disquiet

At the party conferences in the autumn of 2011, Justice for All, the Law Society and other representative groups including the Bar Council spent time with MPs discussing the LASPO Bill, sounding out the possibility of concessions from the government. Justice for All held fringe meetings at all three main party conferences. At the Liberal Democrat conference, James Sandbach from Justice for All told the meeting that the areas of law the government was preparing to take out of the scope of the legal aid system affected the 'most vulnerable in society' and that the proposals amounted to a '66 per cent cut to civil legal aid'. Sandbach said: 'It is disappointing that the government has targeted social welfare law cases as this is the gritty law that affects ordinary people's lives.'

James Sandbach is a policy officer at Citizens Advice with responsibility for legal aid policy. He has good links with the Liberal Democrats and he has been a parliamentary candidate for them. On the Saturday morning of the LibDem conference, in 2011 a resolution critical of the government's plans for the reform of welfare benefits was approved by the delegates. The resolution, which was drafted by Sandbach, argued that claimants going to appeal should be 'given access to adequate support and legal representation'. The Justice for All fringe meeting took place on the Tuesday morning of the conference and the justice minister Lord McNally addressed the meeting dismissing Sandbach's move as a 'Saturday morning resolution, which cannot mean that parliamentarians have to follow it', although he conceded he had to take account of his party's views on the issue.

Speaking to LAG immediately after the fringe meeting Sandbach said: 'Despite the minister's comments it is clear that there is much disquiet among many Liberal Democrats about the impact of the proposed legal aid cuts. Justice for All will hope to build on this to gather support for the bill to be amended once it reaches the Lords.' He was right. It had been rumoured throughout the summer that Tom Brake MP, the Liberal Democrat MP and a government member of the committee, was concerned about the impact of the scope changes on welfare benefits advice.

Brake is a linchpin figure for the Liberal Democrats on legal policy as he chairs the Liberal Democrat Home Affairs, Justice and Equalities Committee. The role of this committee is to act as a bridge between Liberal Democrat backbench MPs and ministers. Soon after the bill was published, Lord McNally had attended a meeting of the committee to be told 'the Bill failed all tests of Liberal Democrat policy'. The MPs were particularly concerned about the impact of the cuts in legal aid for welfare benefits, making the connection with the government's planned reforms of the benefits system. Lord McNally's mood was described as 'grumpy' in the meeting. Lord McNally was reported as having seen a draft of the bill, but he had no influence over its content. Throughout the passage of the bill through the Lords, his heart did not seem to be in the fight and he cut a careworn and increasingly tetchy figure. He was particularly goaded by claims that the bill would have a detrimental impact on Citizens Advice Bureaux. He was prompting to remark in answer to a question from the Conservative Lord Tony Newton at the report stage of the Bill in the Lords:

> One of the few successful things I did when I was in the House of Commons was something that I think cost the then Tory Minister, Gerard Vaughan, his job. He tried to cut Citizens Advice Bureaux funding. I do not know whether the noble Lord, Lord Newton, was a member of the Government who sought to cut Citizens Advice Bureaux funding at the time, but it just goes to show that what goes around, comes around.[5]

At the report stage of the bill before it moved to the House of Lords in November 2011, responding to pressure from his fellow Liberal Democrat MPs, Tom Brake tabled an amendment to bring back complex benefits cases into scope. This was to become the most significant Commons rebellion on the LASPO Bill. Conservative

MPs succeeded in delaying taking the amendment, which meant that Brake was forced into supporting a similar amendment from Yvonne Fovargue, the Labour MP for Makerfield. In her speech she said: 'It is well known that many problems in social welfare law are interconnected and that clients invariably approach agencies with clusters of problems, which is why the social welfare law cluster of housing, benefits, debt and employment was introduced in the first place.' In her constituency she argued that the number of specialists dealing with social welfare law cases would drop from ten to only two if the changes to legal aid were approved by parliament.

Brake argued that the proposal on complex cases was suggested by Citizens Advice which 'has calculated the cost impact of its proposal. It says that the current welfare benefits advice spend is £25 million on just under 140,000 cases, and that restricting it to complex welfare benefit cases covering only reviews and appeals, which applies to two-thirds of the current welfare benefit cases, would cost £16.5 million and help around 100,000 people'. Nine other Liberal Democrat MPs rebelled with Brake and these included the Liberal Democrat Deputy Leader Simon Hughes.

Helen Grant MP was again critical of the government's proposals on domestic violence, arguing that the definition of domestic abuse needed to be more precise and expressing concern about the proposed 12-month time limit on the qualifying criteria in the bill to claim legal aid linked to domestic abuse. She also raised concerns about the exclusion of undertakings as a criterion to qualify for legal aid: 'An undertaking is a legally binding document ... it is specific and clear, and eminently acceptable in my opinion to be part of the criteria.' Again, though, stopping short of outright rebellion she was absent from the chamber when the crucial vote was taken on this. Three Liberal Democrat MPs voted against the government on the amendments on domestic violence.

Sir Bill speaks out

At the end of the 2011 conference season LAPG held their annual conference on 7 October in Birmingham. It was well attended by over two hundred practitioners. The mood was subdued and, unlike previous years, the legal aid minister had decided not to attend. Ironically, given his relationship with some of his constituency officers, Jonathan Djanogly had declined the invitation to run the gauntlet with the assembly of lawyers because of constituency business.

The Chair of the Legal Services Commission (LSC), Sir Bill Callaghan, used the occasion to put down a marker, perhaps with an eye on the Lords stage of the bill. He explained that one of the disadvantages of the government taking direct control of legal aid was the lack of independence in decision-making. Some legal aid clients, he said, such as 'Travellers and terrorists can be politically controversial ... it is very important there is some protection from political in decisions on granting legal aid'. He told LAG when questioned that he believed 'an independent tribunal to appeal decisions on granting legal aid would be the best system'.

Sir Bill Callaghan is not a man to court controversy. Very much a Labour Party establishment figure, having worked as an official for the Trades Union Congress (TUC) he owed his job as chair of the LSC to Labour Party patronage. It was therefore probably as close as he could bring himself to criticising his former political masters in public by saying in his speech: 'I've seen ministers with arms of very different lengths when it comes to decision-making on entitlement to legal aid.' His remarks chime with those anonymous comments made by LSC officials already referred to (see chapter 4).

Preparing the ground

While the LASPO Bill was in the Commons, Justice for All was preparing the ground in the Lords by launching its 'adopt a peer' initiative. Justice for All supporters were encouraged to contact peers who might have local links or an interest in the area of work the agency or firm specialised in. The list of peers adopted by advice organisations and private practice solicitors grew to over three hundred by the end of the campaign. Also, with the help of Lord Bach and the Labour Party's researcher in the Lords, Eva Hartshorn-Sanders, a series of seminars were organised on a non-party political basis to brief peers on the bill.

Part of the Justice for All strategy was to enlist the help of charities without a direct interest in the provision of legal aid services to join the campaign. The disability charity Scope was a charity that played a crucial part in winning over peers. A research report, commissioned by LAG from Scope on the impact of the proposed cuts in legal aid on benefits advice for disabled people was officially launched at one of the all-party seminars in the House of Lords.[6] In the report, Scope followed five typical claimants with disabilities as they negotiated red tape and bureaucracy

6   *Legal aid in welfare: the tool we can't afford to lose,* available at: www.lag.org.uk/ Templates/Internal.asp?NodeID=88856.

to claim benefits, with and without legal aid. The report concluded that, according to the Department of Work and Pensions (DWP), the introduction of the Universal Credit benefit is intended to lift 250,000 households with a disabled person out of poverty, but that many of these people will miss out owing to a lack of awareness over what they are entitled to. Also, the move to transfer more people onto Employment and Support Allowance (ESA) from the 'fit to work' group had been undermined by the DWP's tendency to get these decisions wrong: out of 122,500 appeals heard between October 2008 and February 2010 from people turned down for ESA, almost 40 per cent (48,000) were successful.

Another key member of Justice for All was the National Federation of Women's Institutes, known as the Women's Institute (WI). Sophie Howes, a policy adviser at the WI, sat on Justice for All's steering committee and helped organise the research which led to another report commissioned by LAG, *Legal aid is a life line: women speak out on the legal aid reforms.* The report was published in time for the end of the committee stage of the bill in the Commons in late October 2011. The document drew on academic research and the experience of women who have suffered domestic violence arguing that the proposed criteria to qualify for legal aid 'fail to reflect the reality of women's lives; and in practice will leave vulnerable women without access to legal aid'. In the government's response to the consultation on legal aid reform, it had outlined criteria intended to act as a gateway to qualifying for legal aid in domestic violence cases. The criteria include obtaining a conviction against the perpetrator but, as the WI report pointed out, very few women who are victims of violence are able to do this. A woman who left an abusive partner to live in a refuge told the WI: 'I was with him for eight years, the police had been called so many times, I'd been in and out of hospital because of him, I always dropped charges, I was petrified to take it further.' Many women who spoken to the WI researchers were concerned that they would not be able to gather the necessary evidence to prove domestic violence in order to qualify for legal aid: 'He was a psychopath and I was in intensive care for three weeks and he threatens you doesn't he, that the children will be taken away, so you stay because you're frightened to lose the children, so you stay for that purpose, you get brainwashed. The thing about this is they also rape you, they drag you about, they tie you up, but you may not have the scars, but it's there.'[7] The WI and other women's rights

---

7   National Federation of Women's Institutes, *Legal aid is a lifeline: women speak out on the legal aid reforms*, LAG, 2011.

organisations such as Rights of Women worked together throughout the passage of the bill on briefing parliamentarians on the impact of the government's proposals.

The Law Society also commissioned a paper which was aimed at influencing the debate on the bill. In early January 2012 this research undertaken by King's College London was published. The report, *Unintended consequences: the cost of the governments legal aid reforms*,[8] argued that the three main areas of government cuts of family and social welfare law, as well as clinical negligence, while ostensibly saving £240 million, would lead to unbudgeted costs of at least £139 million. The report's author, Dr Graham Cookson, concluded that the likely budget saving were so low after the knock-on impact of the cuts were taken into account that the research undermined the government's economic rationale for changing the scope of legal aid. This research built on work which had been published the previous year by Citizens Advice[9] – this report, *Towards a business case for legal aid*, had found that £60 million in spending on legal aid in social welfare law cases saved the state £338.65 million in expenditure on other services. In an interview for this book, Citizens Advice Chief Executive Gillian Guy, commenting on this, said, 'It's hard to see who gains by ditching a system (legal aid) that can resolve problems at low cost before they escalate out of control. It simply means the taxpayer has to pick up a bigger bill further down the line'.

Both sides in the debates over the LASPO Bill had made the calculation that it was in the House of Lords that the most opposition to the bill would come. Justice for All and other campaigners had devoted energy to building awareness of the issues around the bill among peers while it was debated in the Commons. The hope was that a large majority of peers would vote in favour of amendments to the bill in order to force the House of Commons look again at these sections again. Justice for All and others opposed to the bill believed that government supporters in the Lords were less susceptible to pressure from the whips and many of the crossbench (non-party political peers), a good few of who are senior lawyers, would be persuaded to vote against the government. With the approval of the bill with some minor government amendments in the Commons, the scene was now set for a clash in the Lords. In keeping with the character of the upper house, this showdown would be heartfelt, as well as intelligent and genteel in tone – more a fall-out in the junior common room as opposed to the gunfight at the OK Corral.

8   Available at: http://soundoffforjustice.org/wp-content/uploads/2012/01/
Kings-College-report-into-costs-of-Govt-legal-aid-reforms1.pdf.
9   Citizens Advice, *Towards a business case for legal aid*, July 2010.

CHAPTER 9

Amendments and concessions

Unlikely rebels

The Legal Aid, Sentencing and Punishment of Offenders (LASPO) Bill received its second reading in the House of Lords in November 2011. The leader of the Liberal Democrats in the House of Lords, Lord McNally, was often the lone defender for the bill, as peers from all of the major parties and the crossbenches subjected it to a verbal shredding. Labour's Lord Bach, Shadow Justice Minister in the Lords, led the attack against the bill, saying that the government had 'failed to get to grips with the serious consequences of their proposed legislation' and that the bill would have 'profound effects on access to justice and people's lives'. Baroness Grey-Thompson, the high-profile former Paralympic athlete and a crossbench peer, said that the proposals in the bill acted as a 'double whammy' for disabled people, who would find themselves without welfare benefits and unable to challenge decisions. Another crossbench peer, Lord Elystan-Morgan, suggested that the provisions in the bill on the criteria to qualify for legal aid in domestic violence cases 'deliberately created a massive obstacle course for likely applicants'. In all, 42 peers spoke against the bill.[1]

Lady Howe, a crossbench peer, reflected the views of many campaigners when speaking in the second reading debate. She said that she would vote against proposals which might give short-term savings, but would lead to greater expenditure in the longer term: 'I need to look at the thing from the point of view, not just what is right or wrong, but what is likely to save money'. Lord Bach agreed with her,

1 January 2012 *Legal Action* 4.

saying 'in the longer term, there will be no savings at all'. Bach also defended the previous government's record, arguing that they had increased expenditure on civil legal aid and appealed to peers to support amendments to the bill:

> The Lords have always had an interest in protecting the rights of those who can't speak for themselves, vulnerable people, poor people. If they are being attacked, the Lords will want to look very carefully ... This is a huge change. They are effectively abolishing social welfare law. To allow it to go through would just be wrong.[2]

After its second reading in the Lords, the bill then moved to the committee stage. In contrast to the Commons, this usually takes place in the main chamber of the House of Lords, but the objective is the same as in the Commons, which is to engage in detailed scrutiny of the bill. Again, much like in the Commons, a tactical game of probing for weakness in the arguments for particular provisions in a bill is played out by introducing amendments, which are debated but not voted on. Voting on amendments is usually saved for the report stage of the debate. Once an amended bill is approved by the Lords, it is passed between the two Houses of Parliament (known as the 'ping-pong' stage) until agreement can be reached on its contents.

Campaigners against the bill were hopeful that more Conservatives and Liberal Democrats would vote in favour of amendments against the government than had done so in the Commons, where the party whips hold more sway. A Liberal Democrat member of the House of Lords willing to be upfront about what might happen was Lord Phillips of Sudbury. Speaking at the launch of LAG's *London advice watch* report in January 2012,[3] he referred to 'disaffection across the House of Lords' over the LASPO Bill and warned: 'There is no question, if the government makes no concessions, there will be votes and the government will lose.' He added that it was 'reasonable to expect major changes at the report stage of the bill'.

Lord Phillips perhaps was not an unexpected potential rebel. He is a former legal aid lawyer, as well as a patron and one of the founders of LAG. Lord Phillips stressed that it was a 'lousy time to be in government' because the economic outlook is so bad and that 'cuts across the board are necessary'. However, in an impassioned speech to an audience of parliamentarians, legal aid lawyers and

---

2   Fiona Bawdon, 'A scorched earth approach to the Legal Aid Bill', March 2012 *Legal Action* 6.

3   Available at: www.lag.org.uk/files/93986/FileName/LondonSWLReportFinal. pdf.

representatives from the not-for-profit sector, he said that 'the cuts have fallen on legal aid harshly' and questioned if it was 'legitimate to deny citizens the means to enforce their right as justice is fundamental to our democracy', and that legal aid spending was a small but an important part of government spending: 'five per cent of defence spending would be enough to fund what is to be cut from legal aid for least three years'.

Lord Carlile QC, another Liberal Democrat peer, told LAG in February 2012: 'There will be a number of votes in which the government will be outvoted.' Lord Carlile seemed frustrated that the government was refusing to make any concessions and had seemingly adopted a 'scorched earth' policy towards amendments to the bill. He warned that the government faced opposition to the bill from its own benches: 'At the moment, there are some grumpy backbenchers around, and I'm one of them.'[4] Lord Carlile had been an outspoken critic of the bill since it was first published. He is a respected lawyer and part-time judge and, like Lord Phillips, his critical view of the bill might have been expected.

However, two more unlikely rebels were the former Conservative cabinet ministers, Lords Tebbit and Newton.[5] They both backed an amendment introduced at the committee stage of the bill to return to scope cases involving children and medical negligence. Lord Tebbit became notorious in the recession of the 1980s for his remark about the riots which had broken out in England in 1981 relating to racial tension and deprivation:

> I grew up in the '30s with an unemployed father. He didn't riot. He got on his bike and looked for work, and he kept looking 'til he found it.[6]

Lord Newton was a less divisive figure than his friend Lord Tebbit. Hugo Young, the *Guardian* journalist, described him as 'a good man, quite outside the nasty brigade'.[7] Lord Newton in a speech on a group of amendments told the House:

4 Fiona Bawdon, 'A scorched earth approach to the Legal Aid Bill', March 2012 *Legal Action* 6.

5 Owen Bowcott, 'Lord Tebbit in fight to save legal aid for children's medical cases', *Guardian*, 19 December 2011 – available at: www.guardian.co.uk/law/2011/dec/19/lord-tebbit-legal-aid-children.

6 Harry Phibbs, 'Iain Duncan Smith is right ... there ARE jobs out there', *Daily Mail*, 7 March 2011 – available at: www.dailymail.co.uk/debate/article-1363808/Iain-Duncan-Smiths-right--ARE-jobs-there.html#ixzz26o0ySHIx.

7 Edward Pearce, 'Conservative cabinet minister who was never "one of us" in the Thatcher years', Lord Newton of Braintree obituary, *Guardian*, 26 March 2012.

> ... when they [the government] come across an amendment with the names Newton and Tebbit on it, they are in trouble.[8]

He went on to argue that the government should look at the names that had been added to the proposed amendments and decide 'that concession was the better part of valour'. Lord Newton was the most outspoken Conservative critic of the government's plans for legal aid. Speaking to an another amendment in the committee stage, he suggested that the planned changes to the benefits system introduced by the Welfare Reform Bill which was passing through the Lords at the same time,

> ... creates a certain amount of turbulence, to put it mildly for a lot of people, including many disabled people and carers. They have great concerns, which may well lead them to want to challenge some decisions. They ought to be able to do so.[9]

Throughout the passage of the bill through the Lords, Lord Newton kept up a thoughtful and principled attack on aspects of the bill which he believed would particularly affect vulnerable people. As a former Social Security Secretary and Chair of the Tribunal's Council (now the Administrative Justice and Tribunals Council) he had a vast knowledge and experience of social welfare law, which fed a strong belief in the value of early legal advice, especially in cases in which people faced the state on the other side. He was gravely ill throughout this period, often relying on an oxygen cylinder in the Chamber while he was speaking in debates, as his lungs were failing. In sticking to his principles by defying the party whips and above all attending debates when he was so ill he demonstrated an inspirational degree of moral and physical courage.

Delays and concessions

In early December 2011 the government announced a delay in implementing its plans for scope cuts. Assuming the bill would be approved by parliament, the cuts would be brought in from April 2013 instead of October 2012. They were forced to do this as the original time-table was too tight. Jonathan Djanogly's effort to implement competitive tendering for criminal legal aid was also officially abandoned, with the government announcing that the first contract will not commence until summer 2015. (Given the record of governments on this

---

8 *Hansard* HL Debates col 377, 16 January 2012.
9 *Hansard* HL Debates col 393, 16 January 2012.

issue and the fact that the preparation for any competitive tendering round would straddle a general election in May 2015, the odds must be stacked in favour of another delay.)

While the bill was in the committee stage in the Lords, the government announced the first two concessions. First, a clause allowing for means testing for legal aid for advice in the police station had been included in the bill, though no one was sure of its origins – this was removed. Second, young adults aged 16–25 were included in the category of clients entitled to legal aid in special educational needs cases. In early March the government also made a partial concession to the Tebbit and Newton demand to continue to allow legal aid in cases involving children under one year old – they said that they would amend the bill when it reached the report stage in the Lords to allow legal aid in obstetrics cases in which children suffer severe brain damage.

At report stage, further concessions were made as pressure had built because of the support from peers across the upper house for amendments hostile to the detail of the government's plans. These concessions included one on domestic child abduction, to allow legal aid to be awarded in cases in which a child had been unlawfully removed from within the UK. Legal aid was also extended to victims of human trafficking to permit them to bring cases against perpetrators of trafficking. The Law Society and expert peers such Lady Butler-Sloss did much of the detailed work in getting these changes to the bill.

A concession for the future

As already discussed, previous governments have used the removal of areas of law from scope as a method of controlling the legal aid budget. Kenneth Clarke and Jonathan Djanogly were engaged in a radical reshaping of the legal aid system and wanted these changes enshrined in legislation to prevent change later down the line and to reduce the potential for judicial review (as courts are reluctant to interfere with primary legislation). According to officials close to them, they wanted to be 'up-front about who would no longer get legal aid' and shared the view 'that people should not go to court'. What they lacked and had no concern for, it seemed, was 'any analysis of what happens if people don't get legal aid'.[10] Clarke was adamant

10 Unattributed Ministry of Justice official.

that he wanted no option for any future ministers to backtrack on his reforms. So, in contrast to previous legislation on legal aid, the LASBO Bill did not allow for areas of law to be added to the scope of legal aid. As originally drafted it was wholly negative, only permitting areas of work to be omitted from the scheme, not added.

Lord Pannick QC, a crossbench peer, was prominent in arguing for the bill to be amended to allow for the addition of areas of law to the scope of the legal aid scheme. LAG understands that this was one of the points raised by Liberal Democrat politicians when holding meetings with Kenneth Clarke to discuss possible compromises to ensure their support. Lord Thomas, a Liberal Democrat peer, let the cat out the bag when responding to a letter from a Justice for All supporter in late February 2012, saying:

> You may know that Liberal Democrat pressure has already achieved a concession from the coalition government that the Lord Chancellor should have the power to place areas of legal assistance back into scope, as well as simply remove areas, as the bill originally stated. Hopefully, that power will be exercised if some of the fears expressed of denial of access to justice come to pass.

Unfortunately for Lord Thomas, the concession had not been announced when he wrote this letter and his actions denied Lord McNally the element of surprise when he eventually announced it to the Lords. Speaking to LAG after LASPOA 2012 became law, Tom Brake MP said he believe the amendment to section 8 of the Act (which defines the scope of 'civil legal services') was important as 'a safety valve to allow government to change tack if some of the predictions about the impact come true'.

The section 8 amendment represented a tipping point between the two members of the coalition government. As discussed below, while the majority of Liberal Democrats seemed prepared to put aside their consciences and vote for the bill, they did not want to close off the hope of a better legal aid scheme in the future when the economy improved, while their Conservative colleagues in government – Clarke and Djanogly – wanted a once and for all redesign.

Lords showdown

By the time the LASPO Bill received Royal Assent in early May 2012, it had suffered 14 defeats in the Lords, the most of any bill in this parliament and a hefty number by the standards of recent history.

The first day of the report stage in the House of Lords set the tone for this series of defeats.

Lord Pannick opened the debate on the amendments, putting forward what LAG believed was an innocuous change to the bill giving the secretary of state the responsibility to ensure access to justice within available resources. Supporting the amendment, Lady Mallalieu QC, a Labour peer, said this would show that the government was 'not abandoning what is an essential pillar of our constitution, which is that nobody should be denied the right to go to a court of law because they can't afford it'.[11] In the first vote on the amendment, the government lost by 45 votes, its biggest defeat in the debate. Much to LAG's surprise, the government resisted this amendment at report stage and throughout the ping-pong stage. When the Commons considered the amendment on 23 April 2012, it was rejected on the grounds of financial privilege and sent it back to the Lords for reconsideration. The Lords did not accept this argument and voted 248 to 233 to reinstate the Pannick amendment to the bill. Lord Pannick eventually withdrew the amendment in the final debate at ping-pong stage. This had the advantage of focusing attention on amendments such as the one on domestic violence which would change scope. LAG assumes the government's resistance to the amendment was that they feared that it might be used in the future to hang a judicial review challenge on.

The Lords did succeed in forcing the government to re-think on the issue of independence in decision-making. The amendment proposed on the first night of report stage concerned the independence of the Director of Legal Aid Casework (DoLAC) and safeguards over the office holder's ability to take decisions on individual cases without fear of interference from ministers. As previously discussed, this had become an issue under the previous government, though it was felt that Ken Clarke would not interfere in cases 'because a) he understood the concept of independence and b) he would not be interested anyway'.[12] LAG and other campaigning organisations believed strongly that a system had to be put in place to protect against political interference from ministers, which was not solely dependent on a future Secretary of State for Justice being principled and/or uninterested. The final Act incorporates a clause on the independence of the DoLAC.

11 Owen Boycott, 'Lords legal aid rebels dig in for five-day haul', *Guardian*, 5 March 2012 – available at: www.guardian.co.uk/law/2012/mar/05/lords-rebels-legal-aid.
12 Unattributed source at the Ministry of Justice.

It was on the second night of debate on the report stage (7 March) that things got more heated than usual in the upper house. At one point in the debate, Lord McNally, facing an onslaught of criticism about the bill from peers, lost his cool somewhat, implying that cross-bench peers were being irresponsible in voting for amendments which were against government. This moved the Conservative peer Lord Cormack to accuse the minister of 'histrionics', which is about as rough has things can get in the usually genteel House of Lords.

Lord McNally seemed particularly grumpy about the amendment on welfare benefits advice which was proposed by the Liberal Democrat peer, Lady Doocey. Justice for All and other charities including SCOPE and Citizens Advice, had lobbied hard for support for this amendment which put back advice on welfare benefits in the legal aid system. Lord Newton also succeeded in a vote on an amendment to return advice on welfare benefits appeals to scope. Lady Doocey withstood a barrage of pressure tactics from government whips to continue supporting the amendment. At report stage her amendment was won by 39 votes, and Lord McNally was moved to say that this and the other amendments approved by peers 'would drive a coach and horses through the bill'.

Peers backed an amendment at report stage from Baroness Grey-Thompson, against the mandatory telephone gateway which the LASPO Bill introduced for the areas of civil law remaining in scope. In proposing the amendment, she said: 'A telephone-only service may work for a large number of people. However, it may adversely impact the most vulnerable clients, who may struggle to explain complex problems over the phone'. She also expressed concerns that the telephone operators would not be legally trained: 'As a result, operators may not be able effectively to interpret the nuances of complex cases put to them, let alone cases put to them by clients who may be confused or have some difficulty in communicating'. The amendment was supported by Lord Newton, who made the point in the debate that 'it is only face-to-face that you can disentangle the points on which they might have a case. This is important to a lot of people who cannot really fend for themselves'. Two weeks after this amendment was won in the Lords, Lord Newton died and the Lords were united in their grief and admiration for this honourable and humane man.

The government eventually made a small concession on the telephone gateway after pressure from solicitors specialising in community care work, but the Grey-Thompson amendment was lost at ping-pong stage. A concession on mesothelioma cases, an industrial disease caused by exposure to asbestos, was agreed also by the government at the last moment in ping-pong stage. It was during the debate on this that the minister Jonathan Djanogly had been pilloried for inappropriate mirth in the debate on the industrial disease mesothelioma (see chapter 6).

Bluster, votes and crossbenchers

Lady Doocey was the exception who stood out among the Liberal Democrat peers, particularly over the amendment on welfare benefits cases. In total she rebelled six times against the government. With hindsight, the rhetoric of Liberal Democrats such as Lords Philips and Carlile can be seen as merely bluster to try to wring concessions from the government. When the crucial votes came on the LASPO Bill, they and most of their colleagues followed the whips. Speaking after LASPOA 2012 was passed, Lord Carlile told LAG that once they had pushed issues as far as they could, they had to bow to the will of the Commons as the elected house. Tom Brake MP insists that there was always limited scope for compromise on this as the fundamental review of legal aid was part of the coalition agreement and so 'it had to be delivered'. He also argues that the bill was part of the deficit reduction plan and so rebellion on the final bill 'was not an option'. During the course of the passage of the bill through the Lords it became apparent to campaigners that despite much sympathy from Liberal Democrat peers, when it mattered they would follow the government whip.

Even Lord Phillips, who had such strong links with the legal aid lobby, was reluctant to defy his party whips. At one point he was going to go through the government lobby voting against an amendment supported by campaigners against the bill when he was forced to take a comfort break. He was verbally assailed in the Lords' facilities by Justice for All campaigner James Sandbach, where Sandbach pointed out to him that if he couldn't bring himself to vote against the government he should at least abstain – which to his credit he did.

Tom Brake readily admits that the issue of legal aid in welfare benefits cases was causing considerable disquiet amongst Liberal Democrat parliamentarians who were exerting as much pressure as they could on Kenneth Clarke to make a concession on this. At the eleventh hour, with the bill in the ping-pong phase, a deal was reached to provide advice and assistance in welfare benefits appeals before the upper tribunal and higher courts. Like so much with legal aid legislation, the devil is in the detail and LAG believes that the government is attempting now to backtrack on this commitment and it seems that much of the efforts of Tom Brake and others who secured the original concession might have been in vain (see the next chapter).

Liberal Democrats were also effectively duped (some might say willingly) by the Conservatives' tactics on the question of financial privilege. At the start of the debate on the LASPO Bill in the Lords, it was asked whether the government would make use of the financial privilege procedure to rule out any amendments by the Lords with cost implications. Lord Strathclyde, the leader of the government in the Lords, argued that designating an amendment as being subject to financial privilege is not a decision which the government takes. While this is correct (it is a decision for the clerks of parliament), he failed to acknowledge that the government decides whether or not privilege is to be waived so that an amendment to a bill made in the Lords can be considered by the House of Commons.

According to the parliamentary clerks, the waiving of financial privilege by governments is a normal part of procedure: 'The Commons waives its privilege far more often than not'.[13] There is also a strong argument that the amendments to the LASPO Bill should never have been covered by financial privilege. According to Jeff King, senior lecturer in law at University College London, financial privilege was wrongly used in the Welfare Reform Bill[14] and if his argument is accepted it also applies more so to the LASPO Bill. This was not a bill directly linked to a finance bill and the sums involved, even if the all the Lords' amendments had been approved by both houses, would have only amounted to a few tens of millions – small change in terms of overall government spending.

While campaigners were disappointed by the support from Liberal Democrats, what was exceptional about the campaign against the bill was the consistent support of cross-benchers. Imran Ahmed was one of the behind-the-scenes figures throughout the passage of the LASPO Bill in both the Commons and the Lords. He is an interesting character. A former Liberal Democrat and ex-medical student who caught the politics bug, he now works for the Labour Party and acted as the conduit for campaigners into the opposition in the Commons and Lords. At the end of the campaign he highlighted the success that lobby groups such as Justice for All had in gaining support

13 *Financial privilege: a note by the Clerk of the House and the Clerk of Legislation.*
14 *Welfare reform and the financial privilege.*

from crossbenchers. He points out that in all of the nine amendments to the legal aid provisions made to the bill at the report stage in the Lords, there is consistently high support from the crossbenchers. For example, on the welfare benefits amendment 90 per cent of the crossbenchers who voted were in favour. In other words, to paraphrase *The Sun* newspaper, as regards amendments, 'it was the crossbenchers wot won them' (see appendix 4).

Domestic violence

Crossbenchers played a significant part in perhaps the most important amendment and eventual concession on the LASPO Bill. As already discussed, family law was the biggest loser from the proposed cuts and of deep concern to many campaigners was the tightening of the rules on qualifying for legal aid for victims of domestic violence. The government feared (and still does) that the cuts in scope for family cases would lead to an upsurge in clients claiming the domestic violence exemption to claim legal aid. The debate in both the Commons and the Lords centred on the definition of domestic violence and the criteria which a victim would have to meet to qualify to claim legal aid.

Rights of Women, the Women's Institute and other campaign organisations wanted the government to use the Association of Chief Police Officers' definition of domestic violence in the bill. This definition has been widely adopted by other organisations, including the Home Office, and defines domestic violence as:

> ... any incident of threatening behaviour, violence or abuse (psychological, physical, sexual, financial or emotional) between adults ... who are or have been intimate partners or family members, regardless of gender or sexuality.

The bill currently used a different definition, referring to physical or mental abuse which includes sexual abuse and 'abuse in the form of violence, neglect, maltreatment and exploitation'.

At the report stage of the bill in the Lords, Baroness Scotland, the former Labour Attorney-General, proposed an amendment which included the Association of Chief Police Officers' definition. Highlighting her concerns, she said: 'In the UK two women every week die as a result of domestic violence. And every week 230 victims need help to leave an abusive relationship.' Baroness Scotland also demanded that the government publish the evidential criteria they were proposing to establish for victims to satisfy to claim legal aid. Baroness Butler-Sloss, a former senior family judge and a crossbench peer, had asked for the criteria to be published before the report stage so that peers could scrutinise them.

The government had realised that it was fighting a losing battle on resisting calls to include the ACPO definition. Speaking to LAG at a meeting in late February 2012 while the bill was in the Lords, Jonathan Djanogly said that it was 'in the mix at the moment' on whether they would concede this, and he also said 'if there is a way of making people happy on this issue [the definition of domestic violence] we will do it'. The following week the government confirmed that they would adopt the ACPO definition. In a last-ditch concession when the bill was at ping-pong stage, the government also widened the criteria to qualify for legal aid in domestic violence cases.

Opponents of the bill were concerned that the government intended to limit legal aid to victims in cases in which the victim had taken successful court action against the perpetrator. Clarke announced to the Commons on 17 April 2012:

> ... we intend to accept as evidence – we will reflect this in regulations – the following matters: an undertaking given to a court by the other party in lieu of a protective order or injunction against that party for the protection of the applicant, where there is no equivalent undertaking given by the applicant; a police caution for a domestic violence offence by the other party against the applicant; appropriate evidence of admission to a domestic violence refuge; appropriate evidence from a social services department confirming provision of services to the victim in relation to alleged domestic violence; and appropriate evidence from GPs or other medical professionals.

The government had moved a long way, including extending the time limit on evidence of domestic violence from one to two years but, as Baroness Scotland said when the issue was debated again a few days later in the Lords, imposing a time limit shows a complete misunderstanding of domestic violence and how victims, usually women, will suffer for some years before finally deciding to take action. Lady Scotland argued that agencies which could provide evidence of domestic violence should not be limited to ones such as refugees, but extended to 'outreach services' such as Citizens Advice Bureaux and that the criteria should include attendance at the matrimonial home by police:

> The noble Lord will know that many victims do not press the matter on to charge or to conviction. The police may have been called many times, but if there is not a charge or a caution, the applicant-victim will not be able to rely on that for legal aid.

Rights of Women's (ROW's) concern remains that regulations need to include those who have not been able to access specialist domestic violence services. Many women are turned away from refuges because of lack of space. A ROW survey undertaken on 16 June 2011 showed that 224 women were refused refuge places: 163 because there were no beds available; 13 because they had no recourse to public funds; and 48 for another reason such as complex needs. Many more women who are victims of domestic violence receive help from other services than are admitted to refuges. ROW and other campaigners including LAG believe that the regulations on legal aid need to reflect the reality of the lives of women and other victims of domestic violence.[15]

In response to the debate in the Lords, the minister Lord McNally listed the initiatives and cash that the government is devoting to services to tackle domestic violence, saying: 'One thing that I am most proud of about this government is that we have put funding into domestic violence issues in a very detailed way'. When Baroness Scotland's amendment had been debated earlier in the week before going back to the Commons, it had won by the narrow margin of 239 to 236 votes. If she had been successful in the vote when it was debated for a third time on 25 April 2012 the government would have had to have accepted her amendment under parliamentary procedure or they would have been forced to ditch the entire bill. The vote was tied at 238 each, meaning that under parliamentary convention the government won the day. Such close votes can come down to the luck of who chooses to attend the chamber at a crucial time. The facts are that no Liberal Democrat or Conservative peers voted for her amendment that night, but 90 per cent of crossbenchers did. It is difficult not to conclude that these politically independent, expert and non-elected parliamentarians got it right and the elected politicians in the Commons, with their party colleagues in the upper chamber, got it wrong.

15 National Federation of Women's Institutes, *Legal aid is a lifeline: women speak out on the legal aid reforms*, October 2011, available at: www.lag.org.uk/ files/93919/FileName/Legal.pdf. Rights of Women and Welsh Women's Aid, *Evidencing domestic violence: the facts*, January 2012, available at: www.row.org. uk/pdfs/Policy/Evidencing_dv_the_facts.pdf.

CHAPTER 10

Austerity justice

Paying the price

The Legal Aid, Sentencing and Punishment of Offenders Act (LASPOA) 2012 received Royal Assent on 1 May 2012. It had taken the coalition government just under two years from the publication of the coalition agreement on 12 May 2010 to introduce legislation to dismantle a large chunk of the civil legal aid system which had evolved since 1949 to provide access to justice for the public. As the final vote on the domestic violence amendment demonstrates, the detail of the eventual act was determined to some degree by a complex parliamentary process in which factors such as luck and political manoeuvres played a part. If one reason had to be cited as an explanation as to how we arrived at this point, then the government's priority to reduce the public spending deficit is it – but the austerity justice system that LASPOA 2012 will create will come at a far higher price than any savings which might or might not accrue from the legal aid budget.

The following table shows the total number of cases which will be no longer receive support from legal aid after April 2013. The figures are taken from the latest impact assessment by the Ministry of Justice.[1] These figures were produced after the Act became law and update the original impact assessment which had been published with the consultation paper in November 2010. The first update to this had been in June 2011.

---

1 *Reform of legal aid in England and Wales: equality impact assessment,* updated June 2012.

Area	Number of cases
Family	232,500
Debt	105,050
Education	2,870
Employment	24,070
Housing	53,200
Welfare benefits	135,000
Immigration	53,290
Other	17,020
Total	**623,000**

Based on figures from the Advice Services Alliance (ASA), LAG had analysed the effect of the cuts at local level for social welfare law (SWL).[2] These figures also reflect the uneven spread of services across the country. For example, because of the work of the charity Law for All (discussed below), Ealing in West London has a proportionately higher level of legal aid services than many similar boroughs both in the London region and nationally. When the cuts are implemented it will lose a total of £1,016,550 in cash for advice on SWL cases. The 'postcode lottery' of legal aid services was well-illustrated by the ASA research, which showed that out of the top five highest spending boroughs for civil legal aid, only Liverpool was outside the London region, whereas areas like Surrey and the East Riding of Yorkshire underspent by a considerable margin what the Legal Services Commission (LSC) estimated would be a fair share of the budget for civil legal aid.[3] LAG's research shows that it will be the poorest boroughs which will be hardest hit by the cuts in SWL legal aid. Appendix 5 shows a table of the top 20 child poverty hotspots and their current spending on SWL legal aid. Tower Hamlets in London tops the list of the hotspots and will lose over £660,000 in funding for SWL cases. This is not highest amount lost by one of these boroughs, but comparisons are difficult due different population sizes and the historic pattern of supply. Overall the table shows that just under £9 million in

2   *Local impact of SWL cuts – table of figures*, available at: www.lag.org.uk/
files/93880/FileName/Copyofswl_impactbyarea_lag.xls.

3   See Steve Hynes and Jon Robins, *The justice gap: whatever happened to legal aid?*, LAG, 2009 p68.

legal aid – which pays for around 5,000 SWL cases – will go from these 20 boroughs and cities which face such severe problems of poverty.

The government's impact assessment on the legal aid cuts paints a grim picture of discriminatory effects of the cuts. For example, they estimate that women will be more affected by the cuts in family law (62 per cent), housing law (61 per cent) and education law (72 per cent).[4] Vulnerable groups of people will also be disproportionately hit. For example, they estimate that 54 per cent of welfare benefits clients cut from scope will have a disability.[5] According to the latest estimate from the Ministry of Justice, the planned cuts will save £410 million, a £60 million increase on their original estimate, with £250 million coming from the changes to scope and £160 million coming from the changes to fees.[6] Ministers knew from the outset that targeting what is a means-tested benefit would mean that it was the very poorest and most vulnerable who would be the biggest losers – it is they who are paying the price of the Ministry of Justice's contribution to the austerity cuts.

The fee changes have been largely absorbed by the sector so far, but according to Carol Storer, the Director of the Legal Aid Practitioners Group: 'For some civil practitioners the 10 per cent fee cut pushed them into deciding to withdraw from civil legal aid. For them the work was already unprofitable and this proved to be the final straw.' For the Law for All charity, a combination of previous fee cuts and the then threat of the 10 per cent cut were factors in them calling in the administrators in July 2011. The charity had dealt with 15,000 clients a year and had received £1.8 million in income from legal aid;[7] it was one of the largest SWL providers. Other specialist advice providers might follow it. The Law Centre Federation estimates that around 50 per cent of the overall income for its 55 members is derived from the legal aid fund. Those Law Centres with a higher portion of their funding from legal aid might well be forced to close their doors when the legal aid cuts hit next year.

At least the not-for-profit sector has the option of raising funds from other sources. The Advice Services Fund previously referred to (see chapter 7) will put £16.8 million into the sector in England and Wales for the next three years (April 2012 to March 2015), though

4 *Reform of legal aid in England and Wales: equality impact assessment* July 2012 p125 – see www.justice.gov.uk/downloads/legislation/bills-acts/legal-aid-sentencing/Royal-Assent-IAs-and-EIAs.zip.

5 *Reform of legal aid in England and Wales: equality impact assessment* p127.

6 MoJ, *Cumulative legal aid reforms*, 13 July 2012 p2.

7 Fiona Bawdon, 'No more law for all', November 2011 *Legal Action* 6.

of course this falls well short of the £50 million it will lose in legal aid income. Private practice solicitor firms do not have the option of charitable funding. Many have been squeezed out of the legal aid system in recent years through a combination of the reduction in the profitability in legal aid and the administrative burden of complying with LSC's contracting conditions. The number of civil legal aid providers dropped by 359 to 1,976 in the last financial year (2011/12). The biggest scope cut (£179 million) is in family law, which is the majority of civil legal aid work.[8] Half or more of these firms could be forced to withdraw from legal aid work. While it is impossible not to acknowledge the difficulties of convincing both the public and politicians that legal aid lawyers are not the money-grabbing fat-cats of the media stereotype, the withdrawal of many firms from legal aid is likely to seriously diminish access to justice for the public.

Family and litigants in person

Throughout the campaign against the coalition government's plans for legal aid, the argument was put that the suggested cuts would not realise the savings that the Ministry of Justice predicted and that there would also be other knock-on costs. This section attempts to paint a picture of the consequences for the main areas of civil law caught in the civil legal aid cuts and give some pointers to the likely future of access to justice for the public.

Due largely to a political consensus around the ending of legal aid from private law family cases, there was little debate over the consequences of this in parliament. Lawyers will also admit, though off the record, that they feel some custody and access arrangement disputes are wrongly prolonged when public funding is available. However, Richard Millar, Head of Legal Aid Policy at the Law Society, argues that by cutting legal aid for family work the government is at risk of 'taking the oil out of the engine, because lawyers make the system [family courts] work'. LAG believes he might have a point.

In August 2012, Mr Justice Ryder, a High Court (Family Division) judge, published his recommendations for reform of the family courts, which include a single family law court, more active case management by judges and the increased use of mediation. He and others, while acknowledging that the system needs urgent reform, are concerned that the cuts in legal aid will lead to a large increase in

8   LSC, *Annual report and accounts 2011–12* p18.

litigants in person who will take up more court resources.[9] Last year there were 109,656 private law family cases – the majority of these will be cut from scope leaving only the public law family cases (see appendix 6).

The numbers of mediated settlements are increasing, according to the family lawyers group Resolution, with 15,319 in 2011/12, up 8 per cent on the previous year[10] – and in one of the few enlightened initiatives from the Ministry of Justice in recent years, they are increasing the cash available for this by £10 million in April 2013. No one in the family justice system disagrees that the government are right to try to encourage mediation in disputes over divorce settlements, custody arrangements and the other legal problems that accompany relationship breakdowns. Many warn though, that there is only so much a change of policy toward mediation can achieve. Those counselling caution include Helen Grant MP, the newly appointed minister in the Ministry of Justice. She made the following observations on the risk of increased litigants in person and mediation in the debate on the LASPO Bill in the Commons:

> The plans rely on judges, magistrates and tribunal chairmen having the time to assist numerous litigants in person, but I can honestly tell Hon. Members that that time does not exist, because judges already have back-to-back lists. Delays in court will become even worse. The plans rely on less dependency on legal proceedings, but as I have said before in the House, mediation is no panacea. It frequently fails, especially in family cases, where there is often an imbalance of power between the parties. Where will all the mediators come from? Who will pay for them?[11]

The courts service is also facing a 25 per cent cut, and so is likely to add to the enormous pressure from litigants in person once the legal aid changes are implemented.

Looking at other common law countries might give a useful insight into what is store in the UK. Bonnie Hough works for the courts service in California. She told LAG that the numbers of litigants in person in child custody and divorce cases has been rising

9   Frances Gibb, 'Obligation for better justice for children', *Times*, 9 August 2012.

10 See Grania Langdon-Down, 'Perfect storm', *Law Society Gazette*, 20 September 2012.

11 Jonathan Isaby, 'Concerns are raised by Tory MPs about cuts to legal aid as Ken Clarke's justice bill gets its second reading', available at: http://conservativehome.blogs.com/parliament/2011/06/concerns-are-raised-by-tory-mps-about-cuts-to-legal-aid-as-ken-clarkes-justice-bill-gets-its-second-.html.

and is currently running at 80 per cent 'and the numbers are going up. Many litigants might start their cases with an attorney and then the money runs out'. In keeping with most of the US, California has a very limited legal aid system which does not cover family cases. According to Hough, the courts system has had to respond to the problem of litigants in person taking up court time by introducing self-help and legal education schemes to assist them. In 2003, for example, $11 million was spent on a system of salaried attorneys to provide support in cases involving child maintenance and other issues related to divorce.[12] LAG is not saying that this is comparable to spending on legal aid in such cases in England and Wales, but what has happened in California illustrates that in the absence of legal aid, the courts system is likely to feel compelled to find solutions to assist litigants in person, which will cost public money. As discussed below, the sort of self-help and legal education services available in the courts in California and may increasingly be seen as a big part of the future in England and Wales, but they do not necessarily lead to better access to justice or savings to the public purse.

Housing

For the public, housing advice comes second only to child protection when they were asked to prioritise areas of work in LAG's opinion poll research.[13] In comparison to the other main areas of SWL of debt, benefits, employment and immigration, less has been cut from housing as the government wanted to preserve scope in cases in which the risk of losing the home was at stake. Unlawful eviction, homelessness, some disrepair cases, injunctions under the Protection from Harassment Act 1997 and possession proceedings will remain in scope. John Gallagher a solicitor at Shelter, the housing charity, believes: 'The most immediate impact is that possession cases based on rent arrears in which housing benefit is an issue. This is the familiar diet of duty solicitor schemes in the county courts.' He fears that while a duty solicitor might be able to get the possession proceedings adjourned, as no one will be able to assist with the problem with housing benefit clients will end up back in court with

---

12 Bonnie Rose Hough, *Description of California courts' programs for self-represented litigants*, prepared for meeting of the International Legal Aid Group, Harvard, June 2003.

13 *Social welfare law: what the public wants from civil legal aid*, LAG, 2012 p7 – available at: www.lag.org.uk/Templates/Internal.asp?NodeID=94036.

nothing resolved. He believes there is a limit to what judges can do in such cases to try to sort out underlying benefits problems: 'Most cases do not involve clear-cut issues, but are factually messy, involving people in and out of part-time work or benefits suspended by the Department for Work and Pensions (DWP) for no discernible reason.'

For private practice housing solicitors, disrepair cases have been the bread and butter of legal aid funded work. Some cases will remain in scope, involving premises which are in such a bad state of repair that there is a serious risk to health and safety and an injunction is needed to get the works done. Russell Conway, a well-known housing solicitor, believes disrepair cases will continue as a counter claim to possession proceedings, along with the higher value cases which some firms undertake in large volumes on conditional fee arrangements, but he says: 'The real problem will be in the case of minor disrepair where the damages will be quite small. Very few firms will be interested in such cases.' Conway predicts that increasing numbers of disgruntled tenants will pitch-up at MP and councillor services.

Legal aid and welfare reform

Second perhaps only to domestic violence cases, the cuts to legal aid for welfare benefits advice proved to the most divisive issue in the course of the LASPO Bill's passage through the parliamentary process. Campaigners and parliamentarians frequently made the link between the implementation of the Welfare Reform Act and the need for advice and representation – this culminated in the government's concession on complex benefit cases described in the last chapter.

Unfortunately for the Liberal Democrats and benefit claimants, they have been out-foxed by the wily Kenneth Clarke and sold a dummy as far as the compromise they reached. In a written ministerial statement issued in September 2012 from another new minister at the Ministry of Justice, Jeremy Wright MP,[14] the government explains that it has not been possible to establish the system of independent verification which it had agreed would identify points of law in cases before the First-tier Tribunal to qualify for legal aid. It has decided to permit legal aid only in cases in which the tribunal itself

14 Ministry of Justice, *Written ministerial statement – legal aid reform*, 18 September 2012, available at: www.parliament.uk/documents/commons-vote-office/September_2012/18-09-12/13-Justice-LegalAidReform.pdf.

identifies an error in its own decision. Paul Treloar, Policy Director at London Advice Services Alliance, says:

> We believe the proposed scheme will cover very few cases and in no way near satisfies what was agreed with MPs. Next year will see massive upheaval in the benefits system due to the introduction of universal credit. Claimants will need expert help particularly with the complex cases these changes are likely to bring in their wake.

As previously discussed, as the welfare state grew, so did the demand for advice on benefits. This was met through a combination of legal aid and, it has to be said, a more substantial contribution from local government and other sources of funding including charitable trusts. The charitable and other services including Citizens Advice Bureaux which grew throughout the last forty years were meeting the demand of the poorest, who are most likely to suffer in economic slumps and the accompanying reshaping of labour markets. The figures speak for themselves on the demand for advice on benefits – 418,000 tribunal claims were received in welfare benefits cases by the tribunal service in 2011 (see appendix 8), nearly half of which were for Employment and Support Allowance (ESA), a benefit for people with disabilities, which will be subsumed into the Universal Credit system in 2013. Also, benefits remain, with advice on debt, the largest source of enquiries for the Citizens Advice Bureaux service with over 2 million annually (see appendix 1).[15]

According to Citizens Advice Chief Executive Gillian Guy, 'The timing couldn't be worse. Legal aid cuts will hit just as the biggest shake-up in the benefits system in more than 60 years gets under way. Welfare reforms already in place – like the switch from incapacity benefit to ESA – have led to a huge surge in the numbers of people needing help and advice. In the last three months alone we saw over 100,000 enquiries about ESA – a rise of a staggering 76 per cent – and over 21,000 of these related to appeals. That's just a small indication of the increased need for advice and support we expect to see when universal credit is introduced. It's no exaggeration to say that the success of welfare reform depends in part on an adequately funded independent advice sector that can both support individuals through the changes and act as an early warning system on where things are going wrong.'

Talking to welfare rights advisers working for local councils as part of the research for this book, they describe services increasingly under pressure as councils are forced to concentrate funds on

15   *Citizens Advice annual advice statistics 2010/11*, available at: www. citizensadvice.org.uk/index/pressoffice/press_statistics.htm.

statutory services. Manchester City Council, which has already been mentioned (see chapter 3), had one of the largest services in England and Wales before cutbacks last year reduced it from 112 to 29 staff, some of whom are paid for by external funders such as the NHS and Macmillan, the cancer charity.[16] Both they and not-for-profit centres are seeing other sources of government funding, such as the NHS services, drying up. According to one welfare rights adviser working for a metropolitan borough council:

> The only reason we are still here is because of welfare reform. Looking at neighbouring councils it's a mixed picture. Some are cutting back but others are taking people on.

Cash-strapped as they are, then, it seems then that some councils are looking to put money into welfare rights services in response to the impending changes in social security law. Unfortunately for clients, it boils down to where they live as to whether they get a service or not.

LAG Immigration and Asylum Law Project

In response to the proposed changes in legal aid in immigration cases LAG has launched its Immigration and Asylum Law Project. Its main purpose is to try and maximise the availability of legal aid and other services to this client group.

Baljeet Sandhu, Solicitor and Co-Director of the Refugee Children's Rights Project based at Islington Law Centre, sits on the steering committee for the project. She foresees potential for challenges under the Human Rights Act, particularly for clients from vulnerable groups such as young people and people with mental health problems. 'Many people will now be left in a desperate state without access to legal aid for immigration advice. The Government seem to believe that social workers can transform into lawyers when necessary and advise young people in their care on immigration issues, asserting that "simple form filling" is required. There is clearly a failure to understand the complex legal issues that often arise in such cases and the experience required to unpack an individual child's case in order to determine what rights and remedies they may have in law.' Baljeet Sandu is also concerned about 'a complete lack of understanding around the impact such proposals will have on the

16 Manchester City Council, *Report for resolution: Citizenship and Inclusion Overview and Scrutiny Committee*, 19 October 2011, available at: www. manchester.gov.uk/egov_downloads/5_Advice_Update.pdf.

duties and responsibilities of already overstretched Local Authorities'. She believes that the 'risks posed to young people and professionals working with them are immense. Proposals such as this are simply knee jerk reactions to try and plug fundamental flaws in the new legal aid regime. Immigration advisors must be regulated and to provide advice whilst unregulated amounts to a criminal offence.'

Many practitioners believe that the government's attempt to withdraw advice completely on non-asylum issues will potentially come unstuck as it is difficult to uncouple interrelated problems within immigration, detention and asylum cases. There are other cases as well in which the withdrawal of legal aid will have unforeseen consequences. Sandu gives the example of cases the Law Centre has dealt with of elderly people who have never regularised their immigration status, but have lived in the UK all of their adult lives without ever knowing that there was a question over their status. She asks, 'What are they supposed to do?'

According to Maurice Wren, the Chief Executive of the charity Asylum Aid, the government's policy of introducing fixed fees in asylum cases has 'incentivised mediocrity at best' as many firms undertaking asylum work to make a profit cut corners. He predicts any further pressure on fees will make a bad situation worse and, like many providers, he believes their will be a greater pressure on finding cash from charitable sources to provide representation in asylum cases.

Access to justice after LASPOA 2012

Optimism was never a plentiful commodity in the legal aid world. Legal aid and other publicly funded legal advice services have always tended to fall short of what legal aid lawyers and advice charities have believed was necessary to ensure that the public got access to the services they needed to advise them and to, when necessary, represent them before the courts. This section discusses some possible ways forward and warns about the likely pitfalls.

Polluter pays

The solution to the availability and funding of advice and representation in benefits cases could be provided by the DWP finding the cash to fund services. As already discussed, transfers have been made in the past from the DWP to cover expenditure on legal aid (see chapter 7). There is also wide support for incentivising departments of state to get their decision-making process right the first time. Charging them for funding advice services is a key component of this. Any 'polluter pays' policy should be linked to the systems thinking approach (discussed in chapter 3) which ensures that repeated mistakes are rectified through appropriate feedback from advice services. One of the failings of the legal aid system has always been that it tends only to look at cases as individual pieces of work. Citizens Advice has a remit to use data from cases to influence social policy, and other not-for-profit organisations undertake this role at both a national and regional level. Joining-up casework and social policy work in a virtuous circle of feedback to government departments to improve services and decision-making should be an aim of any future legal aid system.

One area of SWL in which polluter pays is firmly established as a system of funding advice services is in money/debt advice. A levy on the financial services industry raises just over £80 million which funds the Money Advice Service (MAS). However, only £30 million of this cash goes into frontline services the rest is spent on financial capability education. According to David Hawkes, an expert in money advice policy with Advice UK:

> ... financial capability education is still very new and we do not know how effective it is. Where debt is concerned having to negotiate with creditors is fundamental. Even the most articulate person finds this a challenge and it is an impossible task for the disadvantaged groups which are in the main the clients of not-for-profit advice centres.

Hawkes is also concerned that the present government seems to see the levy on the financial service industry as a way of abdicating their responsibility to fund money advice. He is not alone in pointing out that both national and local government are a major cause of debt problems. With the introduction of the Universal Credit, as well as localising the payment of housing and council tax payments while reducing the amount paid to local government to cover the cost of these benefits, the government is creating the conditions for an avalanche of debt problems for people on low incomes.

The 'universal credit' is the government's flagship policy in welfare reform, and is due to be rolled out next year (2013). It will be piloted in the North East, to be followed by a general roll-out across the country from October 2013. Only new claims will be covered at first, and in the following year existing claims will be transferred to universal credit. The government is calling it 'the most significant change to the welfare system since the Beveridge reforms in 1947'.[17]

17 www.cpag.org.uk/content/universal-credit-universal-panacea.

It will combine benefits such as jobseeker's allowance, income support, family credit and housing benefit into one single benefit. The government's aims by doing this are to simplify the benefits system and to increase incentives for people to take paid employment. With the withdrawal of legal aid for non-housing debt cases and welfare benefits the government are leaving local government and the not-for-profit sector to deal with the consequences of this shake-up of welfare benefits.

Alternatives to legal aid

With welfare benefits there are no alternative options for money to fund these services in the marketplace, but for the other areas of legal aid there are some.

A glimmer of hope for a few clients who will lose out on legal aid is the advent of alternative business structures such as the Co-operative Legal Services. These are likely to provide some increase in the availability of legal services in family and other cases. According to Jenny Beck, Head of Professional Practice at the Co-operative, they have large expansion plans which include employing 3,000 lawyers. Their business will be built on the back of a fixed-fee offering for family law cases, but this is still likely to be beyond the reach of most in the low-income group currently served by legal aid. Also, many clients currently receiving legal aid have complex cases with inter-related social problems such as drug dependency. These are not the sort of clients that it is viable to provide a fixed-fee service to, even if they could afford it.

There exists a well-developed conditional fee ('no win no fee') market in employment tribunal cases – but Richard Dunstan, who covers employment law policy at Citizens Advice, points out: 'Typically our clients have lost a couple of weeks' wages, worth a few hundred pounds – which is a financial disaster for them, but not worth enough for a no win no fee agreement to cover.' Dunstan also argues that while the total number of employment cases covered by legal aid is not large, 'the legal aid contracts pay for a few dozen specialist employment law advisers in bureaux, who act as an expert resource for our volunteers who are dealing with clients who are often low paid but outside the scope of legal aid'.

Rochdale Law Centre has established a Community Interest Company (CIC) which will undertake employment law cases on a no win no fee basis. Clients will be charged 25 per cent of any damages in employment tribunal cases. According to the Law Centre's Senior

Solicitor, Gillian Quine, the service will mainly help those clients who would otherwise not receive a service and produce a small income to help support the Law Centre. The CIC will also charge fixed fees including a fee of £250 for out-of-country visas and other applications in immigration cases. Immigration practitioners say that many families will find the cost of paying for their cases by cutting back on other family expenditure such as food and fuel. Julie Bishop, the Director of the Law Centres Federation, sums up the general feeling among all practitioners about the increasing use of fixed-fee services: 'No one is under any illusion that this is a solution to replace legal aid. It is not, as it will not change the fact that the people who got help from legal aid got it because they could not afford to pay for legal advice.'[18]

While dismissing the idea that voluntary groups and pro bono lawyers can fill the gaps left by legal aid, Law Society President Lucy Scott-Moncrieff does acknowledge the potential for an increase in pro bono activity to assist in some cases. She has suggested better collaboration with City law firms to take on strategic cases against public bodies, and recently announced the Law Society's intention to work with students at Northumbria University to draft standard letters to GPs to help in benefits cases. 'We are trying to make sure that decisions are not appealed so that claimants don't need a lawyer', she says.[19]

No one in the pro bono community claims that they can replace legal aid. A well-connected City lawyer who prefers to remain anonymous met Jonathan Djanogly after the consultation paper had been released, partly to tell him this. According to the lawyer, Djanogly readily agreed that pro bono would not replace legal aid, but Djanogly 'just did not believe that the sorts of cases being cut needed expert legal help. The real question here is why the government does not seem to care about the gaps that will be left in access to justice for people with housing, benefits and other problems'.

Telephone and internet services

The government's 'telephone gateway' (the telephone service legal aid clients will have to pass through) came under fire in the House of Lords especially. The government is, however, pressing ahead with its

18 'Rochdale pioneers: innovations in the not for profit sector', September 2012 *Legal Action* 7.
19 Catherin Baksi, 'Society unveils access to justice initiatives', *Law Society Gazette*, 2 February 2012 p3.

implementation. It will initially cover only special educational needs, debt and discrimination cases, but the government intends to roll it out to cover more of the areas of law which remain in the scope of legal aid. LAG has consistently supported telephone advice services, and in *The justice gap* we argued for 'a national telephone advice service supported by comprehensive legal materials available online'.[20] What is becoming clear from research, though, is that while these sorts of services are increasingly available, they do not necessarily serve those who will lose out when the legal aid cuts are made.

Legal Services Research Centre (LSRC) research on telephone advice found that clients from vulnerable groups, such as those suffering from an illness or disability, were more likely to use face-to-face services. They also found considerable differences in the outcomes achieved for clients between face-to-face and telephone services.[21] Elizabeth O'Hara, Policy Officer at housing charity Shelter, says that this research accords with Shelter's experience of providing face-to-face, telephone and internet advice services: 'We have a website service which receives thousands of hits a day, but it is largely not used by the people who use our face-to-face Housing Advice Centre services. People are not channel shifting between different types of services.' Shelter believes that more tangible outcomes are associated with face-to-face services and that while the government believes that telephone services are cheaper to provide, housing advice on the phone actually takes longer.[22]

LAG's opinion poll research found that 43 per cent of people used the internet to obtain advice, and that the usage was higher in younger age groups.[23] However, the LSRC has found that while internet sites increased young people's knowledge of the law, this does not give them the confidence or ability to pursue their case.[24] The availability of online resources, then, might assist in some cases, and more generally raise people's awareness of what their legal rights are, but it cannot be assumed that it would will replace traditional face-to-face services.

20 *The justice gap* p138.
21 Balmer, Smith, Denvir and Patel, 'Just a phone call away: is telephone advice enough?' *Journal of Social Welfare and Family Law*, Volume 33, Issue 4.
22 Shelter, *Policy Briefing: Shifting channels – Housing advice and the growth of digitisation* 2012.
23 *Social welfare law: what the public wants from civil legal aid*, LAG, March 2012, available at: www.lag.org.uk/Templates/Internal.asp?NodeID=94036.
24 Catrina Denvir, 'Caught in the Web?' Legal Services Research Centre University College London, unpublished, 2012.

Exceptional cases – some room for optimism?

As already discussed, one of the main reasons that the coverage of civil legal aid has been reduced in the way it has is that government's intention was to create a scheme that only intended to provide the minimal level of service necessary to protect human rights. To this end, the 'exceptional cases' rule contained in LASPOA 2012 s10 is intended as a human rights safety net and was used by the government as reassurance to critics that despite the draconian scope cuts, human rights in civil law would be protected. An optimistic view is that the clause could turn out to be a foundation stone on which a rather more substantial legal aid scheme is constructed than the government might have intended.

Miles, Balmer and Smith, in their recently published research paper, argue that a much larger proportion of civil cases than the government's estimate of 5 per cent might qualify for legal aid under section 10.[25] They conclude that 56.6 per cent of family clients might be considered to have a treated or treatable mental health problem, and this could bring many potential cases under the qualifying criteria if a court deems that under article 6 of the European Convention on Human Rights (eg right to a fair trial, including access to legal representation) legal aid is necessary to give a convention right 'practical effect'. What is meant by 'exceptional' is not clearly defined, and as the impact of the changes to scope play out, judicial opinion might begin to favour an interpretation of the word 'exceptional' as meaning cases in which the mental stress the participants are subjected to risks breaching their human rights if they do not have access to legal advice and representation.

However substantial the section 10 safety net system becomes, it will not get any way near to covering the bulk of cases cut from the scope of the legal aid scheme. At best what is likely to happen is that the existing firms that specialise in mental health, community care and human rights build up the numbers of cases they undertake on legal aid certificates through the exceptional cases rule. The service will be patchy and very dependent on good referrals, especially in those geographical areas without a specialist firm or not-for-profit organisation.

---

25 'When exceptional is the rule: mental health, family problems and the reform of legal aid in England and Wales' (2012) 24 *Child and Family Law Quarterly* Issue 3.

Problem clusters

Much of the early part of this book was devoted to telling the story of how legal aid and specifically civil legal aid developed in a very piece-meal fashion. Until the introduction of quality marks and compulsory contracts the patter of provision was determined by where solicitors chose to establish their practices. For various reasons, including social change and the fact that it suited the solicitor private practice model, civil legal aid was mainly concentrated in family law, while other areas of law were neglected or confined to a few niche firms. It has been one of the themes of LAG's 40 years of work in access to justice policy that legal aid services needed to expand to better cover other areas of civil law. Under Lord Mackay, from 1996 (the year the non-for-profit legal aid franchising pilot scheme was introduced), a process commenced in which the not-for-profit sector was encouraged to contract to provide SWL services and the LSC through its procurement strategy, began to try to better co-ordinate the provision of family and social welfare law services. This policy shift was informed by the idea that people, especially the poor and vulnerable, tend suffer these problems in clusters.

Though not perfect, the current system at least provides a common system of funding and quality standards. When it works well, the legal aid scheme allows for the diagnosis of the cluster of inter-related civil legal problems a client might be facing and gives the client the combination of solicitor firm(s) and not-for-profit organisations to deal with these. The necessity to find budget cuts, combined with the notion that civil legal aid had expanded to cover areas of law in which advice and representation is unnecessary, has led to a change of policy. Post LASPO some clients might receive a service, if their case fits:

1) the restricted scope of the legal aid scheme;
2) a fixed- fee offered by a legal services provider; or
3) if it is of sufficient merit and value, to be worth the risk of a no win no fee agreement.

Alternatively, a client might get help from a charitable or pro bono legal service provider, but again this is likely to be in stand-alone areas of law such as benefits, and it will be dependent on local factors such as an enlightened local council willing to fund advice services. Non-specialist and non-lawyer services might also be restricted to giving some information and self-help support, but not the assistance the client needs to obtain an effective remedy to their problem. LAG fears

LASPOA 2012 will lead to Balkanised collection of disparate services with large gaps in between.

A vision of the future

The immediate future is likely to be messy as it always is when major change hits legal aid. These are the main problems that are immediately foreseeable:

1) The government will try to continue its squeeze on fees in civil and criminal legal aid. In doing this it will risk losing the talented and experienced from the sector, resulting in more miscarriages of justice and failures to protect human rights.
2) The 'exceptional cases' rules are likely to prove a happy hunting ground for public law specialists, and it will be some time before the boundaries of what is in or out of scope are established, leading to uncertainty over the legal aid budget and for clients and potential clients over what is covered by the legal aid scheme.
3) It should not be underestimated the sheer potential for unexpected pitfalls in the byzantine tendering processes that the LSC and its successor body the Legal Aid Agency run. The Law Society's judicial review success demonstrated the potential for this.
4) For the not-for-profit sector there will be closures and consolidations as agencies struggle with the twin challenges of increasing demand and dwindling resources.

By taking over direct control of the administration of legal aid, ministers have no hiding place from the problems outlined above. The LSC politically acted as a buffer between the legal aid lawyers and the government, as well as a convenient scapegoat when things went wrong. The problems of administering a complicated system, with a difficult to control budget and the added layers of complexity which being part of the justice system brings, will all now be directly those of ministers. So, for example, if a judicial review is lost due to a flaw in procurement procedure this might lead to calls for the Secretary of State for Justice's resignation, as might budget overspends.

So far, so pessimistic, but at its lowest ebb the seeds of recovery for the legal aid system and access to justice in general might have been sown. In the research for this book it has become apparent that many in the Liberal Democrats are unhappy about what they see as fundamentally un-liberal policy of cutting off the means of redress for many people when faced with legal problems caused by the state and other large institutions. Liberal Democrat MP Tom Brake openly admits that the policy goes against that of his own party and that the Liberal Democrat manifesto might well look to reverse the worst of the cuts. Individual Conservative MPs are known to be unhappy about the impact on family and other cases. Also, the move to create the advice services fund shows they are aware that the cuts to not-for-profit organisations will cause problems (maybe an institutional memory of the Vaughan affair[26] is in play here?). While Labour will make no spending commitments to put back areas into scope, they continue to be vocal about the loss of SWL especially.[27]

Former legal aid minister Lord Bach admits that if Labour had remained in power cuts to legal aid for family law would have been likely, but he argues 'the coalition government made fundamentally the wrong choice in cutting social welfare law and offering insufficient protection for the victims of domestic violence'. He believes if Labour had remained in power they would have found savings by introducing competitive tendering for criminal cases and reducing fees in very high cost criminal cases such as fraud trials. When questioned by the author he would not say if Labour would find the cash to restore legal aid for social welfare law and some family cases if they returned to power, arguing this is a decision which would have to taken nearer the general election.

LAG is launching a commission on SWL around the same time that this book is published with the express intention of trying to influence the political party's election manifestos for the 2015 election. This and other initiatives need to continue to highlight the impact of the loss of legal aid and other services which provide access to justice, so that the politicians are forced to respond to the problems the current government's policies have caused.

Pointers to the future

Sketching out the ideal policy for access to justice is a work in progress. LAG's commission will play a part in this, as will other policy initiatives and research. To conclude this contribution to the debate about the future of access to justice policy, here are five suggested priorities for policy makers and a final thought on public opinion.

26 See page 36
27 See: www.lawgazette.co.uk/news/no-turning-back-cuts-under-labour-says-khan?utm_source=emailhosts&utm_medium=email&utm_campaign=GA Z+02%2F10%2F2012.

1) Independence in decision-making

The new rules to prevent interference in decisions on entitlement to legal aid in individual cases are not robust enough to prevent real or perceived political interference. As discussed in chapter 5, there was concern among officials about the actions of former ministers, an independent tribunal system needs to be established to adjudicate in such decisions.

2) A review of the impact of the cuts

This needs to be held before the general election in 2015 and scope restored (under LASPOA 2012 s8) for those areas of law in which the withdrawal of legal aid has caused substantial hardship to people and significant knock-on costs to the justice system and other arms of the state.

3) End the postcode lottery in civil legal advice services

A theme which has run through this book and indeed much of the research and policy thinking on legal services is the uneven spread of services. This is set to increase with changes introduced by LASPOA 2012 and the other cutbacks in legal advice services. At the very least there should be co-ordinated mapping of legal need.

4) Re-thinking funding legal aid services

Ideas such as polluter pays and compensating the legal aid fund for external cost-drivers such as the knock-on costs in the criminal justice system have been doing the rounds for some time, along with alternative sources of funding such as the levy on client account interest. The problem has been the lack of political will to implement them. A future government will need to revisit them if it is to be serious about ensuring access to justice in the civil justice system.

5) A Minister for Access to Justice

In discussing the LASPOA 2012 debate, one of the most disheartening themes is the government's – and most specifically, the Ministry of Justice's – seeming indifference to access to civil justice. The very basic right of a citizen to be able to get advice on and if necessary enforce their rights in civil law, has been sacrificed for budget cuts of dubious merit in terms of overall money saved. The priority of making sure people obtain meaningful redress with legal problems needs to be reasserted at the heart of the government and justice system. To do this, and to co-ordinate access to justice policy, LAG would suggest that a post of Minister for Access to Justice needs to be created at the Ministry of Justice.

Public opinion

Legal aid and not-for-profit advice services will adapt to the changed funding environment. There will be painful cuts, firms and advice centres will close or be forced to merge, and many experienced and able lawyers and advisers will be obliged to move on to other work, which is a shameful waste of expertise. It will be the poorest and most vulnerable groups in society who will suffer most from the austerity justice system which will be the legacy of this coalition government.

Research to inform policy makers and public opinion about the impact of the cuts will be vital in the coming years. Providing analysis and comment on policies will be equally important, as the government should be held to account for effectively turning back access to justice 40 years for large swaths of civil law. The campaigns around LASPOA 2012 did start to raise this concern with the wider public, but they were often drowned out by the policy priority of addressing the public spending deficit. Economic prosperity ebbs and flows, but an essential cornerstone of a democratic state should be a justice system that provides effective redress and equality before the law for all its citizens regardless of means. Making this argument in the court of public opinion in the coming years is what will ultimately determine whether the low point which LASPOA 2012 represents is permanent or not.

APPENDICES

Breakdown of advice delivered at Citizens Advice Bureaux

The tables below break down the total number of enquiries in Citizens Advice Bureaux nationally for the year 2011/12. Figures are taken from the Citizens Advice 'Advice Trends' publication quarter 4.

Advice delivered by bureaux – England & Wales	Annual 2011/12	% change from 2010/11
Total number of people helped with new or ongoing problems*	2.0 million	−2%
of whom clients with new problems	1.9 million	−2%
Percentage from black and ethnic minorities (average of last 4 quarters)	15.4%	+0.3 percent point
Total number of client contacts – ie, interactions	5.5 million	−5%
Total problems	6.9 million	−3%

---

* A client is counted once only in a quarter, however many times s/he returns. Client and contact totals and corresponding changes are now adjusted to remove a small amount of double-counting.

Problems by category	Annual 2011/12 (thousands)	% of total problems	% change from 2010/11
Benefits and tax credits	2253	33%	4%
Debt	2138	31%	−6%
Employment	524	8%	−8%
Housing	489	7%	−3%
Relationships and family	320	5%	−6%
Legal	268	4%	−11%
Signposting and referral	144	2%	−15%
Financial products and services	129	2%	−2%
Consumer goods and services	120	2%	−11%
Immigration and asylum	83	1%	−13%
Utilities and communications	82	1%	−9%
Health and community care	74	1%	−5%
Tax	59	1%	−11%
Travel and transport	47	1%	−9%
Education	26	0%	−15%
Other	100	1%	10%

www.citizensadvice.org.uk/index/aboutus/publications/advice_trends.htm

Breakdown of visitors to the Citizens Advice online advice service

The tables below break down the number of visitors to the Citizens Advice online service. Figures are from the Citizens Advice 'Advice Trends' publication quarter 4.

'Adviceguide' use – UK	Annual 2011/12	% change from 2010/11
Total number of visitors	11.52 million	+22%
Total number of visits	13.37 million	+24%
Total page views – content*	21.64 million	+18%

* Page views include content pages, factsheets and FAQs, but Introduction and Index pages are excluded. Scotland and Northern Ireland content-specific pages have been included since 2010/11.

Page views by category	2011/12 (thousands)	% change from 2010/11	% of total page views
Benefits and Tax Credits	4,301	–2%	20%
Consumer goods and services	2,409	33%	11%
Debt	2,253	29%	10%
Discrimination – all	274	123%	1%
Education	414	62%	2%
Employment (excl. discrimination)	4,025	11%	19%
Health	2,265	28%	10%
Housing	601	18%	3%
Legal	1,888	30%	9%
Family	1,892	45%	9%
Tax	1,323	–2%	6%
Total views	21,645	18%	100%

www.citizensadvice.org.uk/index/aboutus/publications/advice_trends.htm

Comparison of court-related spending in EU countries

Table from Roger Bowles and Amanda Perry, *International comparison of publicly funded legal services and justice systems*, Ministry of Justice, October 2009.

	Legal aid spend per capita (LA)	Spend on courts per capita (C)	Public prosection costs per capita (PP)	Sum of court-related spend per capita (LA+C+PP)	GDP per capita (Euros)
France	4.68	36.32	10.40	51.40	26,511
Germany	5.68	n/a	n/a	n/a	26,754
The Netherlands	23.2	46.81	20.58	90.61	29,993
Sweden	10.57	51.32	9.85	71.74	28,832
England & Wales	57.87	8.09	14.52	80.48	24,579

Legal aid provisions in LASPO Bill

Analysis of votes on the amendment to the legal aid provisions in the LASPO Bill at the report stage in the Lords (source Imran Ahmed, Labour Party researcher).

| 1 | **Pannick (CB)** Woolf (CB) Faulks (Con) Hart of Chilton (Lab) | DUTY TO MEET CITIZENS' NEEDS The current bill does not contain any duty on the Lord Chancellor to provide the services the bill permits him to provide. This would ensure the Lord Chancellor has to meet the needs of citizens within the resources available and the scope of legal aid as defined by the bill. | 45 Majority. 83% of Crossbenchers voted with us. Rebels were: Faulks (Con), Newton (Con), Carlile (LD), Doocey (LD), Maclennan (LD), Taverne (LD), Thomas of Walliswood (LD) |

3 4	**Pannick (CB)** Woolf (CB) Faulks (Con) Hart of Chilton (Lab)	INDEPENDENCE OF DOLAC With the abolition of the Legal Services Commission, a new Director of Legal Aid Casework, reporting into the Lord Chancellor, will decide who gets legal aid and who doesn't. These amendments would ensure that when making decisions the Director acts independently of the Lord Chancellor. In criminal law, this ensures the Lord Chancellor can't both be responsible for prosecuting someone and for deciding if they get a lawyer to defend them. Similarly in social welfare law the Lord Chancellor is a member of the Government. As such, they have a vested interest not to provide advice on challenges to another Government department.	17 Majority. 70% of Crossbenchers voted with us. Rebels were Newton (Con), Linklater (LD), Phillips (LD)
4	**Grey-Thompson (Cross)** Bach (Lab) Newton (Con) Pannick (Cross)	TELEPHONE GATEWAY Ensures that the telephone gateway the Government intend to make the mandatory entry point to the legal aid system is not mandatory. Urgent and complex cases or those with large amounts of documentation will be difficult to resolve over the phone. Clients who do not speak English will also struggle. Research by Legal Action Group has shown that the groups most likely to experience a social welfare law problem are also those least likely to use a telephone helpline. The Legal Services Research Centre and UCL have recently published research into telephone advice for housing problems. It reveals that under-18s; clients with illness or disability (especially those with mental health issues); and people facing homelessness, especially those with housing benefit problems, are much less likely to use the telephone than face to face services.	28 Majority. 82% of Crossbenchers voted with us. Rebels: Newton (Con)

2 192 194 196	**Scotland (Lab)** Butler-Sloss (CB) Blair of Boughton (CB) Bishop of Leicester	DOMESTIC VIOLENCE EVIDENCE Private family legal aid allows women and men to resolve contentious disputes on divorce, custody and ancillary relief (finances, etc.) through the courts where absolutely necessary. The Labour Party support the Government's aim of restricting private family legal aid in a time of austerity to cases where abuse has been present. However, despite a last minute announcement of a u-turn on the description of domestic abuse, we disagree on what evidence it will accept as proof of domestic abuse. The amendment ensures acceptable evidence reflects best practice across the Government, integrating the government's list of acceptable evidence with the UK Border Agency's list of acceptable evidence for the purposes of immigration.	37 Majority. 84% of Crossbenchers voted with us. No rebels.
168	**Doocey (Lib)** Newton (Con) Bach (Lab) Pannick (Cross)	WELFARE BENEFITS – TRIBUNALS These amendments would ensure there is funding for Citizens Advice Bureaux, advice charities and some faith groups to provide advice on reviews of decisions, appeals to the First Tier Tribunals. 80% of these appeals are applying for disability benefits where there is a degree of subjective analysis involved. Appellants have a 78% higher chance of succeeding if they are advised.	39 Majority. 87% of Crossbenchers voted with us. Rebels: Newton (Con), Stewartby (Con), Avebury (LD), Carlile (LD), Doocey (LD)
169	**Bach (Lab)** Pannick (Cross) Alton (Cross) Newton (Con)	WELFARE BENEFITS – HIGHER COURTS These amendments would ensure there is funding for specialist Welfare Benefits lawyers to provide advice on appeals to the Upper Tribunals on a point of law, and advice and representation on appeals to higher courts including the Supreme Court.	28 Majority. 90% of Crossbenchers voted with us. Rebels: Newton (Con), Avebury (LD), Carlile (LD), Doocey (LD)

171	**Grey-Thompson (Cross)** Benjamin (LD) Eaton (Con) Newton (Con)	CHILDREN SOCIAL WELFARE This would ensure that for those children that do not have an adult to help them through the civil justice system in matters relating to their social welfare, they will be provided with advice and, where appropriate, representation. The Government contends 95% of children will have an adult there to help them. That is no argument for not providing help to the other 5%.	12 Majority. 79% of Crossbenchers voted with us. Rebels: Cormack (Con), Eaton (Con), Stewartby (Con), Benjamin (LD)
172	**Cormack (Con)** Eaton (Con) Crisp (Cross)	CHILDREN CLINICAL NEGLIGENCE This would ensure that for children under 18, clinical negligence proceedings are funded through legal aid. It is widely recognised that the cheapest way to fund clinical negligence is legal aid because (a) rates are limited and (b) there are no success fees or ATE insurance. The state is, of course, the defendant in these cases.	13 Majority. 87% of Crossbenchers voted with us. Rebels: Cormack (Con), Eaton (Con)
170	**Lloyd of Berwick (Cross)**	CLINICAL NEGLIGENCE DISBURSEMENTS This would ensure that poor litigants get an expert report (required before ATE insurance can be purchased) paid through legal aid, providing evidence of negligence.	6 Majority. 97% of Crossbenchers voted with us. Rebels: Newton (Con)

Child poverty hotspots in England, 2010

Rank		Number of Cases Cut				
		Debt	Housing	Bens	Emp	Total
1	Tower Hamlets	578	716	2020	360	3674
2	Islington	263	450	500	200	1413
3	Hackney & City of London	930	1235	2770	380	5315
4	Newham	908	842	1830	230	3810
5	Manchester*					
6	Westminster	330	396	610	100	1436
7	Camden	443	608	1400	250	2701
8	Haringey	263	425	770	100	1557
9	Barking & Dagenham*					
10	Nottingham	848	518	1210	100	2676
11	Enfield	150	104	210	100	564
12	Birmingham	1590	1231	3640	100	6561
13	Hammersmith & Fulham	203	270	380	100	953
14	Lambeth	338	486	900	100	1824
15	Liverpool	1875	900	6270	750	9795
16	Brent	473	619	1670	130	2892
17	Waltham Forest	375	191	600	100	1266
18	Southwark	293	418	820	110	1640
19	Middlesbrough	300	184	530	100	1114
20	Leicester*					
GRAND TOTAL		10155	9594	26130	3310	49189

* These are Community Legal Advice Service areas. The total approximate spend is given for each of these areas. Most of this will be lost if the scope cuts are implemented

Loss of Funding to Legal Aid Providers					CLAS Funds
Debt	Housing	Bens	Emp	Total	
£115,500.00	£124,653.60	£337,340.00	£82,800.00	**£660,293.60**	
£52,500.00	£78,300.00	£83,500.00	£46,000.00	**£260,300.00**	
£186,000.00	£214,855.20	£462,590.00	£87,400.00	**£950,845.20**	
£181,500.00	£146,577.60	£305,610.00	£52,900.00	**£686,587.60**	
					£1,495,375
£66,000.00	£68,904.00	£101,870.00	£23,000.00	**£259,774.00**	
£88,500.00	£105,861.60	£233,800.00	£57,500.00	**£485,661.60**	
£52,500.00	£73,915.20	£128,590.00	£23,000.00	**£278,005.20**	
					£516,607
£169,500.00	£90,201.60	£202,070.00	£23,000.00	**£484,771.60**	
£30,000.00	£18,165.60	£35,070.00	£23,000.00	**£106,235.60**	
£318,000.00	£214,228.80	£607,880.00	£23,000.00	**£1,163,108.80**	
£40,500.00	£46,980.00	£63,460.00	£23,000.00	**£173,940.00**	
£67,500.00	£84,564.00	£150,300.00	£23,000.00	**£325,364.00**	
£375,000.00	£156,600.00	£1,047,090.00	£172,500.00	**£1,751,190.00**	
£94,500.00	£107,740.80	£278,890.00	£29,900.00	**£511,030.80**	
£75,000.00	£33,199.20	£100,200.00	£23,000.00	**£231,399.20**	
£58,500.00	£72,662.40	£136,940.00	£25,300.00	**£293,402.40**	
£60,000.00	£31,946.40	£88,510.00	£23,000.00	**£203,456.40**	
					£456,000
£2,031,000.00	**£1,669,356.00**	**£4,363,710.00**	**£761,300.00**	**£8,825,366.00**	

Family matters

Matters affecting children: Number of children involved in public and private law applications, made in each tier of court by HMCTS region, 2011[1,2]

Region	Public law			
	Family Procedings Court	County Court	High Court	Total
London	3,112	1,700	114	4,926
Midlands	3,647	784	59	4,490
North East	4,428	746	42	5,216
North West	3,041	809	56	3,906
South East	4,557	1,163	43	5,763
South West	2,337	886	53	3,276
Wales	1,337	567	11	1,915
England & Wales	22,459	6,655	378	29,492

Source: HMCTS FamilyMan system and summary returns.

Notes:
1 Figures relate to the number of children subject to each application.
2 Private Law applications exclude adoptions.

Region	Private law[3]			
	Family Procedings Court	County Court	High Court	Total
London	1,057	14,517	418	15,992
Midlands	5,726	13,930	86	19,742
North East	1,583	16,453	99	18,135
North West	2,648	12,573	74	15,295
South East	2,140	19,598	86	21,824
South West	2,529	9,815	91	12,435
Wales	3,754	2,460	19	6,233

3 Special Guardianship Orders figures in the Family Proceedings Courts are only available for those courts which share premises and administrative systems with county courts. The total has therefore been estimated based on the proportion of the total public law and private law applications made in each tier of court.

Government's estimate of reductions in legal aid*

Reduction in legal aid for customers (by spending) 2008/09 rounded to the nearest £1m

LSC Statistical Category	Legal Help		Legal Representation	
	Reduction in spend (£m)	Proportion of existing spend	Reduction in spend (£m)	Proportion of existing spend
Combined Family	n/a	n/a	n/a	n/a
Financial Provision	n/a	n/a	n/a	n/a
Help with Mediation	n/a	n/a	n/a	n/a
Other Family Matters	n/a	n/a	n/a	n/a
Priv. Law Children Act	n/a	n/a	n/a	n/a
Total Family	**50**	**82%**	**128**	**41%**
Actions Against Police	1	53%	1	19%
Consumer	1	100%	4	78%
Education	1	98%	0	29%
Clinical Negligence	1	100%	16	86%
Community Care	0	0%	0	0%
Debt	16	75%	1	43%
Employment	4	100%	0	82%

* Goverment's estimate of reductions in *Legal Aid Reform: Scope Changes*, Impact Assessment (IA No 028), November 2010, p17.

LSC Statistical Category	Legal Help		Legal Representation	
	Reduction in spend (£m)	Proportion of existing spend	Reduction in spend (£m)	Proportion of existing spend
Housing	7	31%	5	17%
Immigration	12	29%	6	16%
Miscellaneous	0	755	4	45%
Personal Injury	0	0%	0	0%
Public Law	0	0%	0	1%
Welfare Benefits	22	100%	0	49%
Total Civil	**64**	**43%**	**37**	**34%**
Grand Total	**114**	**54%**	**165**	**23%**

Social security and child support

Receipts and disposals by benefit type 2010–11

Benefits	Receipts	Disposals
Attendance allowance	4,200	3,600
Disability living allowance	79,400	65,100
Bereavement benefit	500	480
Carer's allowance	1,600	1,300
Child benefit lone parent	1,900	1,800
Child support allowance	3,700	3,600
Tax credits	3,000	2,800
Credits (other)	5	–
COEG	–	–
Compensation Recovery Unit	370	340
Housing/Council tax	12,300	12,300
Disability working allowance	–	–
Employment support allowance	197,400	176,600
Health in pregnancy grant	390	480
Home responsibilities protection	25	30
Incapacity benefit	34,300	37,400
Income support	15,100	15,700
Industrial death benefit	–	–
Industrial injuries disablement benefit	9,200	8,100

Benefits	Receipts	Disposals
Job seekers allowance	47,000	43,100
Lookalikes	8	6
Maternity benefits/allowances	230	230
Others (extinct/rare benefits)	140	79
Penalty proceedings	–	–
Pensions credit	1,600	1,700
Retirement pension	960	870
Severe disablement benefit/allowance	130	120
Social fund	4,800	4,500
Vaccine damage appeals	7	8
Total	**418,500**	**380,200**

Source: http://www.justice.gov.uk/downloads/statistics/tribs-stats/annual-tribunals-statistics-2010-11.pdf.

Index

165